THE ART OF
READING
MINDS

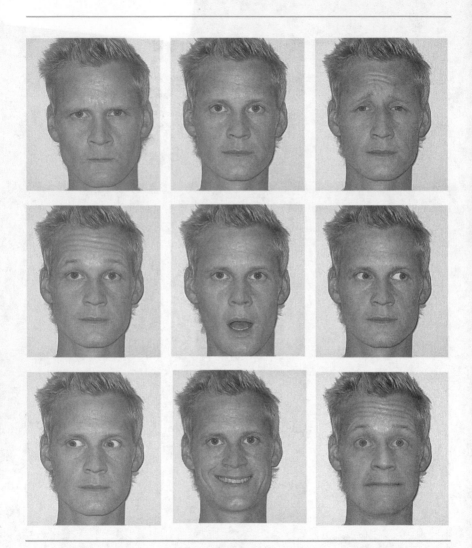

THE ART OF
READING
MINDS

How to Understand and Influence
Others Without Them Noticing

HENRIK FEXEUS
Translated by Jan Salomonsson

ST. MARTIN'S
ESSENTIALS
New York

First published in the United States by St. Martin's Essentials, an imprint
of St. Martin's Publishing Group

THE ART OF READING MINDS. Copyright © 2019 by Henrik Fexeus,
by agreement with Grand Agency. Translation copyright © 2019
by Jan Salomonsson. All rights reserved. Printed in the
United States of America. For information, address St. Martin's Publishing Group,
120 Broadway, New York, NY 10271.

www.stmartins.com

Pages 51–52: Photographs by Anders Karlsson
Page 64: Photographs and photomontages by Anders Karlsson
Pages 96–104, 106–109, 111–113, 115, 118, 121, 123:
Photographs by Olof Forsgren
and Anders Karlsson; photomontages by Anders Karlsson
Page 123: Photographs by Pressens Bild

The Library of Congress Cataloging-in-Publication Data is available upon request.

ISBN 978-1-250-23640-1 (trade paperback)
ISBN 978-1-250-23641-8 (ebook)

Our books may be purchased in bulk for promotional, educational,
or business use. Please contact your local bookseller or the Macmillan Corporate and
Premium Sales Department at 1-800-221-7945, extension 5442, or by email at
MacmillanSpecialMarkets@macmillan.com.

A different version of this book was published in 2007 in Sweden under
the title *Konsten att läsa tankar* by Bokförlaget Forum and was later published in
English by Stockholm Text in 2012.

First St. Martin's Essentials Edition: October 2019

10   9   8

For my children
Sebastian, Nemo, and Milo,
who help me realize every day how much
I still have to learn about communication

Contents

Preface to the Updated Edition   ix

A WORD OF WARNING   xiii
A Reminder Not to Take Things Too Seriously

1. MIND READING!?   1
A Definition of the Concept

2. RAPPORT   10
What It Is and Why You Want It

3. RAPPORT IN PRACTICE   19
Using Unconscious Communication Consciously

4. SENSES AND THINKING   58
How Our Thoughts Are Determined by
Our Sensory Impressions

5. EMOTIONS   80
How We Always Reveal Our Emotions

6. IT'S NEVER TOO LATE   133
A Moral Tale About the Importance of Reading Minds

7. BE A HUMAN LIE DETECTOR   136
Contradictory Signs and What They Mean

8. THE UNCONSCIOUS PICKUP ARTIST   161
How You Flirt with People Without Even Knowing It

9. LOOK DEEP INTO MY EYES . . .   174
Methods of Suggestion and Undetectable Influence

10. HAUL ANCHORS   194
How to Plant and Trigger Emotional States

11. SHOW OFF   212
Impressive Demonstrations and Party Tricks

12. MIND READING!!   230
Some Final Thoughts About What You've Learned

References   235

Preface to the Updated Edition

Welcome, dear reader, to this brand-new edition of *The Art of Reading Minds.*

Since you and I are new to each other, a short background might be in order. My interest in human behavior and psychology started in primary school. In my attempts to socialize with the other children, I had a constant, nagging feeling that everybody else had received a manual titled *How to Interact with Others,* and that I had been at home the day it was handed out. I was socially awkward, to put it mildly, until seventh grade. And, of course, this meant that I got picked on a lot, which in turn meant that I started to ask myself some questions: How did my behavior differ from that of others? Why did my antagonists act as they did? *What influenced our actions—and interactions?*

I have spent most of my adult life trying to find the answers to these questions. I looked for pieces to the puzzle in diverse fields, such as theater, advertising, philosophy, media, psychology, and religion. As a result, I accumulated a fairly extensive understanding of human behavior, and eventually I combined it with my love of magic. I became what is referred to as a "mentalist." Outside of the world of TV dramas, a mentalist is someone who combines psychology with trickery and misdirection to create the illusion that he or she is able to read minds and influence others on a supernatural level. I used my knowledge purely for entertainment, because I didn't think that anyone else was interested in the "real" workings of human behavior. I thought everyone already knew. Turns out I was wrong—again.

I was soon asked to give talks about body language and nonverbal communication. The original version of this book was an attempt to expand on those first talks. As I said, I thought it would interest only a handful of people. That handful turned out to be half a million readers, from all corners of the world, who have read the book in thirty-five different languages. (More than a decade and countless lectures later, I am still in something of a state of shock over this fact.)

I am immensely proud that St. Martin's Press is now presenting *The Art of Reading Minds* to you and other readers in the United States. To celebrate this, I have completely revised and updated the book, creating a version that has never before been published. I do hope you'll enjoy it.

—Henrik Fexeus, Stockholm, 2019

Once Upon a Time . . .

A Word of Warning

A Reminder Not to Take Things Too Seriously

'd like to make something clear. I don't claim that the contents of this book are objectively "true" as such, at least no more true than any other subjective views of the world. These are simply theories and ideas that a lot of people put their faith in and that seem to hold water when measured and tested. But there are several competing worldviews that make precisely the same claim when it comes to representing "truth," such as Christianity, Buddhism, and science. So although the contents of this book are useful tools, they are really no more than metaphors, or explanatory models, if you prefer, that describe reality as seen a certain way. Different people prefer to use different models to make sense of their realities. Some label their models as religious, others call them philosophical, and others still call them scientific. Which category the metaphors in this book ought to be placed in would depend greatly on whom you're asking. Some would consider them scientific. Others would argue that psychology and psychophysiology are not sciences. Some would criticize the models in this book and call them overly simplistic generalizations of complex phenomena, unworthy of anybody's attention. I would disagree, because these specific metaphors, these models, have proved to be unusually useful tools for understanding and influencing other people. This doesn't mean that they describe things the way they objectively "really are." In the field of psychology, the ground is constantly shifting, and today's truth might turn out to be tomorrow's lies—only to be regarded as true once more the day after that. The only claim I make is that if you apply the things you are about to learn, the results will be very—*very*—interesting.

1

Mind Reading!?

A DEFINITION OF THE CONCEPT

*In which I explain what I mean by "mind reading,"
what it was that Descartes got wrong, and our
journey together begins.*

I believe in the phenomenon of mind reading, completely and wholeheartedly. For me it's no more mysterious than being able to understand what someone is saying when she is talking to me. The fact is that it might actually even be a little less mysterious than that. There is nothing particularly controversial about mind reading, as far as I'm concerned. In actual fact, it's completely natural—something we all do, all the time, without realizing it. But, of course, we do it to varying degrees of success and with more or less awareness. I believe that if we know *what* we are doing and *how* we do it, we will be able to train ourselves to do it even *better*. And that's the point of this book. So what is it that we actually do? What do I mean when I say that we read each other's minds? What does "mind reading" actually mean?

To begin with, I want to explain what I *don't* mean. There's something in psychology that is referred to as *mind reading,* and it's one of the reasons why so many couples end up in therapy. This happens when one person presumes that the other person can read her mind:

"If he really loves me, he should have known I didn't want to go to that party, even though I agreed to go!"

Or:

"He doesn't care about me, or he'd have realized how I felt."

Such demands for mind reading are more like outbursts of ego-centricity. Another version of this is supposing that you can read someone else's thoughts, when you're actually just projecting attitudes and values from your own mind onto hers:

"Oh no, now she's going to hate me."

Or:

"She must be up to something—why else would she be smiling like that?"

This is called *Othello's mistake.* None of these things are mind reading in the sense that I am talking about here. They're just foolish behavior.

Descartes's Big Mistake

In order to understand mind reading as I am about to describe it, it is important that you first understand a different concept. The philosopher, mathematician, and scientist René Descartes was one of the great intellectual giants of the seventeenth century. The effects of the revolution he instigated within mathematics and Western philosophy are still being felt today. Descartes died in 1650 of pneumonia in the Royal Palace in Stockholm, where he was tutoring Queen Christina. Descartes was used to working in his warm, cozy bed, as befits a French philosopher, so the cold stone floors of the castle quite understandably finished him off once winter set in. Descartes did a great deal of good, but he also made some serious mistakes. Before he died, he introduced the notion that body and mind were separate. This was pretty much the most stupid thing he could have come up with, but Descartes had won the ear of the intelligentsia, thanks to neat sound bites like *Cogito, ergo sum* (I think, therefore I am). As a result of his popularity, the peculiar (and basically religious) notion that human beings are made of two different substances—a body and a soul—gained ground.

There were naturally those who thought he was wrong, but their voices were drowned out by the cheers of celebration for Descartes's idea. Only in recent times have biologists and psychologists been able to scientifically prove the exact opposite of Descartes's claim; perhaps the most notable among them is the world-famous neurologist Antonio Damasio. Now we know that the body and mind are actually inextricably linked, in both the biological and the mental senses. But Descartes's view was dominant for so long that it is still taken as an accepted truth by most people. Most of us still differentiate, albeit unconsciously, between our bodies and our thought processes. If the rest of this book is going to make any sense to you, it is important to understand that this isn't the case, even if it feels a bit strange to think this way at first.

Here's how it is: you can't think a single thought without something physical happening to you as well. When you think a thought, an electrochemical process occurs in your brain. In order for you to create a thought, certain brain cells have to send messages to each other according to certain patterns. If you have had a thought before, the pattern for it is already established. All you're doing then is repeating the pattern. If it is an entirely new thought, you create a new pattern or network of cells in your brain. This pattern also influences the body and can change the dissemination of hormones (such as endorphins) throughout your body, as well as in the autonomous nervous system. The autonomous nervous system governs things like breathing, the size of our pupils, blood flow, sweating, blushing, and so on.

Every thought affects your body in some way or other, sometimes in a very obvious way. If you're frightened, your mouth will go dry and the blood flow to your thighs will increase in preparation for possibly running away. If you start to have sexual thoughts about the guy at the supermarket checkout, you'll notice other, very obvious reactions in your body—even if it is only a thought. Sometimes the reactions are so small that they're invisible to the naked eye. But they are always there. This means that by simply being observant of the physical changes that occur in a person, we can get a good idea of how she is feeling, what her emotions are, and what she is thinking. By training yourself at observation, you will also learn to see things that were previously too subtle for you to notice.

Body and Soul

But it doesn't stop there. Not only are all our thoughts reflected in our bodies; the reverse is true as well. Whatever happens to our bodies affects our mental processes. You can easily test this yourself. Try the following:

- Clench your jaw.
- Lower your eyebrows.
- Stare at a fixed point in front of you.
- Clench your fists.
- Stay like this for ten seconds.

If you did this right, you might soon feel yourself starting to get angry. Why? Because you've just performed the same muscle movements as your face does when you are feeling *angry*. Emotions don't only happen in your mind. Just like all our other thoughts, they happen in the whole of our bodies. If you activate the muscles that are associated with an emotion, you will activate and experience that same emotion, or rather, the mental process—which will in turn affect your body. In the test you just did, you activated your autonomous nervous system. You might not have noticed it, but when you did that test, your pulse increased by ten to fifteen beats per minute, and the blood flow increased to your hands, which are now feeling warmer or itchy. How did that happen? By using your muscles as I suggested, you told your nervous system that you were angry. And presto!

As you see, it works in both directions. It makes complete sense, when you think about it—anything else would actually be pretty peculiar. If we think a thought, it affects our bodies. If something happens to our bodies, it affects our thoughts. If this still doesn't seem to make sense, that could be because we usually refer to some kind of incorporeal process or sequence with the word "thought," whereas the word "body" is used to refer to a physical entity. Another way of describing it in more straightforward terms is this: you can't think anything without it having some effect on your biological processes. These processes don't just occur in the brain, but in the whole organism. In all of you. In other words, forget Descartes.

Wordless and Unconscious

The mental and biological parts are two sides of the same thing. If you understand that, then you're already well on the way to becoming a fantastic mind reader. The basic idea of mind reading, as I use the term, is to gain understanding of other people's mental processes by observing their physical reactions and features. Of course, we can't "read" what goes on inside their minds in any literal sense (to begin with, this presupposes that everyone thinks in words, and we will find out that this isn't always the case), but we don't actually need to, anyway. As you are now aware, seeing what is happening on the outside can be enough to allow you to understand what is happening on the inside. Some of the things we observe are more or less fixed: physical stature, posture, tone of voice, and so on. But many things change constantly as we speak to someone: body language, eye movements, tempo of speech, etc. All of these things can be considered "nonverbal," or wordless, communication.

The fact is that the majority of all communication that takes place between two people occurs without words. What we communicate with words is sometimes just a fraction of the total message. (Even collaborating to solve a mathematical problem requires a certain amount of nonverbal communication, if only to get the problem solvers motivated to work together.) The rest is communicated with our bodies and the quality of our voice. The irony is that we still insist on paying the most attention to *what* someone is saying to us—in other words, which words the person chooses to use—and only occasionally consider *how* it is said. To put it another way: wordless communication, which constitutes a huge chunk of our total communication, doesn't only happen without words. Most of it also happens unconsciously.*

What's that? Surely we can't communicate without being aware of it? Well, actually we can. Even if we look at the whole person

---

* To be precise, the voice is described as *intraverbal* communication, in contrast to body language, which is nonverbal. To make things easier for myself, and to help keep this book portable, I have decided to bundle them together under the heading *wordless communication*.

we are talking to, we almost always pay the most attention to the things she's saying to us. How she moves her eyes, her facial muscles, or the rest of her body are all things we don't often pay attention to, other than in the most obvious of cases. (Like when someone does what you just tried doing: lowering the brow, clenching the jaw, and staring with clenched fists.) Unfortunately, we're also pretty useless at picking up on what people are saying to us with their words; we are constantly exposed to loads of hidden suggestions and ambiguous insinuations that slip straight past our conscious minds. But they do a little dance with our own unconscious mind, the far-from-insignificant part of us where a lot of our opinions, prejudices, and preconceptions of the world are stored.

The truth is that we always use our entire bodies to communicate, from enthusiastic hand gestures to changes in the size of our pupils. The same is true for how we use our voices. Although we are often bad at consciously picking up the signals, our unconscious mind does it for us. All communication, regardless of whether it happens through body language, smell, tone of voice, emotional states, or words, is absorbed, analyzed, and interpreted by our unconscious minds, which then send out suitable responses through the same wordless, unconscious channels. So not only do our conscious minds miss most of what people are saying to us, we also have very little notion of the responses we are giving. And our unconscious, wordless responses can easily contradict the opinions we believe ourselves to hold, or whatever we are expressing in words. This unconscious communication obviously has a great impact on us. It's the reason why you get the nagging feeling that somebody who seemed very nice in conversation didn't actually like you. You have simply picked up hostile signs on an unconscious level, and they are now forming the basis of a perception whose origin you cannot fathom.

But our unconscious minds aren't flawless. They have a lot to take in, understand, and interpret, all at the same time, and nobody has taught them how to do it. So they often make mistakes. We don't see everything, we miss nuances, and we misinterpret signs. We end up in unnecessary misunderstandings.

That's why this book exists.

You already do it, but you could do it better.

Together, we're going to take a look at what we're really doing, wordlessly and unconsciously, when we communicate with other people. And what it means. To get to be as good as possible at communication—and reading minds!—it is important to learn to pick up and correctly interpret the wordless signs that people around us give off unconsciously when they communicate with you. By paying attention to your own wordless communication, you can decide what message to communicate, and make sure that you're not misunderstood because you gave off ambiguous signals. You can also make things easier for the person you are communicating with by making use of the kinds of signs that you know the person will most easily pick up. If you use your wordless communication the right way, you will also be able to influence those around you to make them want to move in the same direction as you and to attain the same goals as you. There's nothing nasty or immoral about this. You already do it. The difference is that you don't currently have any idea what messages you're sending out or what effect you're having on the people around you.

It's time to change that. And I really mean it. My goal is to give you this knowledge in as easy, straightforward, and practical a way as possible.

I just bought a new bunk bed for my children. From IKEA. If

it had come with an eleven-page instruction manual that spent the
first ten pages explaining why beds are great to have, and then concluded with, "You already have all the tools you need to make your
own bed! Just get to work! Make sure you have a solid frame! And
don't forget a comfortable mattress!" I would have been pretty angry and poked the first IKEA employee I came across in the eye
with an Allen key. But I've noticed that there are a lot of books that
do just that. They spend the whole book promising to explain how
to achieve something or other, but you're none the wiser after
you've finished reading them. You still have no idea of what to do
in purely practical terms in order to become a better person (this is
often the point). Or how to join the stinking headpiece to the joist,
for that matter. I hope this book isn't one of those books.

I want this book to be as clear and straightforward as an IKEA
instruction sheet. Once you've read the book, you'll understand
what I've been talking about, in concrete and practical terms. You
will begin practicing different methods of mind reading and ways
of influencing other people's thoughts while you read it. You'll
know where the headpiece goes. And you won't even need an Allen
key.

One last thing: nothing in this book was discovered by me. Everything you're going to read is based on and collated from works by
the true masters of the various fields discussed. The real work was
done by people like Milton H. Erickson, Richard Bandler and
John Grinder, Desmond Morris, Paul Ekman, Ernest Dichter,
Antonio Damasio, Erika Rosenberg, William Sargant, Philip
Zimbardo, William James, Denise Winn . . . to mention only a
few. Without them, this book would have been a very quick read.

I hope you are sitting comfortably. Let's get started.

2

Rapport

WHAT IT IS AND WHY YOU WANT IT

*In which we discuss cycling and how to
establish a good relationship with anybody you like
without uttering a word.*

There is a very good reason why we want to know what somebody else is thinking: it helps us establish *rapport*. It's an internationally acknowledged term, used in the realm of wordless communication, and that is why I will be using it here. Rapport is something we always try to establish with the people we meet, whether it is in a business context, where we want people to understand our presentation of an idea, or simply in a case of wanting the attention of the hottie in the checkout line at the supermarket we were fantasizing about just a few pages ago. In both of those cases, we can only succeed by establishing rapport.

The word "rapport" comes from the French term *le rapport,* which means *to have a relationship with*, or *connection to*, someone or something. By establishing good rapport, we are creating a relationship of mutual trust, consent, cooperativeness, and openness to each other's ideas. Sounds useful, huh?

Rapport is the basis for all meaningful communication, at least when you want the person in question to listen to and care about the things you have to say. When you're trying to deliver a message, even if it's simply an attempt to get your kids to empty the dishwasher, if you haven't ensured that you're in good rapport with the person you're talking to, you might as well not bother. The person won't listen to you anyway. Rapport is also a prerequisite for people liking each other on a more personal level. *How* personal is up to you, but without rapport there's no point even trying.

We are always establishing good and bad rapport with the people around us. By learning how it's actually done, you can learn how to always make good rapport, even with people you wouldn't ordinarily get along with. Funnily enough, you often come across these people holding positions in which their decisions or attitudes concerning your opinions and ideas can greatly influence your future. Wouldn't it be nice if he or she understood what you mean for once?

I understand if you can't see how rapport has anything to do with mind reading, but I have to insist that it does. What you will learn to observe in others, in order to establish rapport, will also tell you where they are mentally, how they understand the world, what they're thinking, and how they feel. Mind reading begins at that early stage, as a condition for creating good relationships.

The Basic Rule of Rapport

The basic rule for establishing rapport is really very simple, but it's based on a deep insight into how people work. The basic rule of good rapport is to *adapt to how the other person prefers to communicate.* (If you've studied marketing, you have been taught to always communicate on the level of the target demographic. Same thing.)

You do this in a variety of ways, which we shall soon go through. They are, almost without exception, wordless methods that the person you are communicating with will only pick up unconsciously.

By adapting to someone else, you achieve two different things. It makes it easier for the other person to understand what you're saying, since you are expressing yourself (wordlessly) just like she would have done. The recipient no longer has to "translate" your wordless communication into something she better understands, as you are now communicating in the way that she prefers (and understands the best). When the person you are talking to no longer has to "filter" your information to understand it, that means that the danger of misunderstanding has been minimized. To be able to adapt to another person, you first have to make sure you understand *how* she prefers to communicate. In other words, by learning to observe how other people communicate, you're also learning to understand what they are actually trying to say. The other thing you accomplish is making her like you better. The reason for this is simple: by adapting to the other's way of communicating, and becoming the same, you show that *you are like him or her,* since your expressions resemble that person's. And people like people who remind them of themselves. Who do we like the best of all people? Ourselves. This only makes sense, after all, as we are the only living beings we can ever know from the inside. (This is also the reason for the so-called "spotlight effect," a concept proposed by psychologists Thomas Gilovich and Kenneth Savitsky, which states that we tend to believe that others notice us more than they actually do.) The rest of the world is only accessible to us by observation, which creates an emotional distance. By the same logic, then, the answer to the question of who we like second best seems obvious: we like people who are like us. We like to spend time with people who are like us, who see the world the same way we do and who like and dislike the same things we do. Research has shown that we also prefer to hire people who are like us. A recent study by the Gallup organization found that one of the most important things for a new employee is "good rapport and trust between the immediate supervisor and the employee."

We choose our closest friends based on who makes us feel comfortable being the way we are. And who better for that than people who are already like us?

At this point I feel a brief comment is in order. The idea of adapting to somebody else is, naturally, not for you to completely erase your own personality. Establishing rapport in this way is something you do *initially,* when you've just met somebody. In any relationship or encounter, we adapt to each other, back and forth, once good rapport is established. You can help this procedure along by establishing rapport consciously, by selflessly offering to be the one to adapt, as you are likely to be more aware of the procedure than the person you're meeting with. It's not really any stranger than offering to speak a few words in a foreign language to somebody who understands it better than English. You adapt to the way the other person prefers to communicate. By adapting to somebody else, by beginning to speak his language, even if not fluently, you're telling the unconscious mind, "I'm like you. You're safe with me. You can trust me."

After rapport is established, you can start changing your own behavior to achieve the same changes in the other. Once you're in rapport, you don't need to keep following the other person's lead or adapting to her; she'll gladly follow you. That's just how rapport normally works. We take turns following each other's leads, all the time.

I promise you, somebody who speaks his own language better than English will both have an easier time understanding you and like you better if you don't insist on speaking English exclusively. But as soon as this person has decided he likes you, he won't mind giving his own broken English a try.

If you're in good rapport, the person you're in it with will have an easier time accepting your ideas and suggestions, too. When somebody likes you, she tends to want to agree with you. This means that if you adapt to a person and show her that you are like her, she will feel an urge to agree with you. The things you say are the kinds of things she could have thought of herself (since you are so alike). Disagreeing with you would be a little like disagreeing with herself.

Once you're in rapport, you can also take the lead and bring the person you're with to a positive mental state, one better suited for clearly understanding your message or ideas and the value of them. This is a case of influence without control. We're not trying to manipulate anybody in any sinister sense of the word. If your idea isn't actually any good, it won't convince anybody, no matter how good your rapport is. What we want to do is to create a relationship in which you can creatively and constructively discuss any issue with respect and understanding. We don't "control" or deceive other people to give them opinions they don't really hold. We just make sure that they are in an optimal state to understand the actual advantages of whatever we are presenting, using only simple means, such as moving our bodies or adjusting our voices according to certain principles.

If I am the same as you, you will understand and like me. If you like me, you will want to agree with me.

Situations in Which You Need Rapport

It's never too late to start establishing rapport with somebody. Perhaps you have a very bad relationship with someone and want to change that. Start establishing rapport the next time you meet. You probably won't manage to turn things around in one go, but if you keep trying to establish rapport every time you meet, you'll notice a big difference in how the other person acts toward you fairly soon. Then, of course, there arc always a few people that it would simply seem impossible for you to create good rapport with. Usually, you don't really want to, anyway, so that's OK. I'm not saying you *have to* be in good rapport with everybody you meet. I'm simply saying it *can* be done.

When is rapport useful? Pretty much always. I mentioned some situations earlier. Communications expert Elaina Zuker lists some other everyday situations:

- When you want to finally understand what the person you've been living with all these years is trying to tell you.
- When you're trying to regain some of the respect your teenage kids have lost for you.
- When you're dealing with bosses, teachers, government agencies, or any other type of authority.
- When you come across people whose service you need but who can cause you problems, such as an ill-tempered bank clerk or a stressed-out restaurant waiter.

- When you receive a sales call (in this case, you might prefer to be going for bad rapport).*
- In any type of situation where you are being assessed or judged, such as a job interview.

Zuker also offers the following examples from professional life:

- You often need to achieve more, with fewer resources. Often, you'll find yourself competing with your colleagues, and your work might depend on your ability to establish rapport with important people—like the person in charge of the resources.
- To be a successful executive today, you need expert-level people skills. If you "go your own way," you might risk alienating both your higher-ups and the people who work under you.
- If you want to convince people of your innovative idea, you need a well-developed set of communication skills. Your amazing idea won't be going anywhere unless you can convince the right people.
- When you're in the middle of an organization, you have people above you that you report to, and others that you are expected to lead. To get the results you want, you need to be able to create good relationships both above and below you.

---

* All of these techniques can be used the other way round, to destroy rapport (you will notice how some people you have a hard time getting along with are true masters of this art). All you need to destroy rapport is to use methods for communication that are as far removed as possible from those used by the other person. Bad rapport is an efficient way of finishing off a meeting quickly or making bothersome people leave you alone. You simply make yourself too troublesome and unpleasant for them to want to continue talking to you.

- In flat organizations, you often end up with more responsibility than actual power. You have to work through other people to get things done, which can only be achieved by establishing rapport and working together.
- All of the things your years of work experience have taught you don't mean as much as your ability to establish rapport. No matter how skilled you are, nobody wants an expert who is impossible to talk to.

Perfecting What You Already Know

Remember, you already use most of the mind-reading techniques I will touch on here. You just don't know it. Also, you probably don't use them to their maximum effect. What we're going to do is take a look at these techniques, sharpen them up to make them effective, and then put them right back into your unconscious. And since you already know all this stuff in some sense, there's no reason to feel daunted by the amount of information and number of techniques in the pages that follow. The fact is, you'll have an easier time learning this than a lot of other skills. Here's a model of how the learning process works:

- **Step 1: Unconscious Ignorance** The classic example is riding a bike. In step 1, that means you don't know how to ride a bike, but you also don't know there is any such thing as cycling.
- **Step 2: Conscious Ignorance** You don't know how to cycle, but you are aware of cycling and that it is something you are ignorant of.
- **Step 3: Conscious Knowledge** You can ride a bike, but only when you concentrate and focus on what you are doing.

- **Step 4: Unconscious Knowledge.** You can ride a bike, and you don't even have to think about it to do it.

Real learning only happens at step 4, and you're already there. However, we're going to return to step 3 to polish your skills, and maybe we'll add a thing or two to them. Getting back to step 4 will be your job, and you have all the time in the world to do it. After you've done the exercises in this book, start using the methods one at a time until you notice yourself doing each of them automatically (i.e., you've reached step 4). Only at that point should you begin using another method. Don't try to do everything at once; you'll only get confused. Take your time, and remember to enjoy yourself! It really is a lot of fun, especially once you begin to realize how easy it is and how well it works.

3

Rapport in Practice

USING UNCONSCIOUS COMMUNICATION CONSCIOUSLY

In which you learn how to use body language and other wordless methods to achieve your ends, in a completely different way than you might expect.

Now, take a deep breath. In the next few pages, I will be bombarding you with facts, methods, and techniques that can be used to establish rapport. You'll learn about everything from body language and tone of voice to energy levels and personal opinions. Of course, the whole idea is for you to use these ideas in real life, and the sooner you begin practicing, the better. However, you must remember not to rush through them. Take your time to learn to master the different methods.

You won't have to worry about "getting caught" while you're practicing establishing rapport with people. I promise you, nobody will complain about how you've become easier to understand and more pleasant to converse with, or even that you suddenly seem to be able to read their minds. Although, for a time, you will be very aware of everything you do, the same doesn't go for the people around you.

Shake That Booty!

How to Use Body Language

As I mentioned earlier, we establish rapport by adapting to our recipient in a number of different areas. The first of these is body language. I am actually not particularly fond of that term. "Language" makes it sound as though there's a vocabulary list somewhere that you can just learn. Of course, books like that do exist. They teach you that when someone's little finger is held in a certain way it means one thing, and when her left foot does a particular thing, it means something else. But things aren't quite as simple as that. Our gestures don't always mean the same thing in every situation or for every person. To write an entry in a dictionary of body language that says that crossed arms mean "keeping one's distance / dissociation / doubt"—which I know a lot of people would happily write—is wrong, on the one hand because it ignores the considerably more multileveled and dynamic expressions our bodies can make, and on the other hand because it seems to require you to believe that body language exists in isolation, independent of all other things. You must have crossed your arms at some point and been struck by the thought, "Right! This is what people do when they're angry or keeping their distance. But I'm not angry!?" Exactly. There may have been some other reason: perhaps it was cold and you crossed your arms to stay warm. Or it was just a convenient way for you to rest your arms for a minute. To make sure if someone is really keeping his or her distance or being doubtful, we have to look for other visible physical signs and consider the context in which these gestures are being carried out. How does the rest of the body look? Are the arms tense or relaxed? What about the face? Has your discussion been heated? Is the room cold? And so on.

I would prefer to replace the term "body language" with something else, like "bodily communication." But that sounds pretty dry, too. And since I don't want to cause confusion by adding yet another new term to an area that is already overburdened with terms and definitions, I'm going to stick with "body language"— which, as you've come to understand, is a term for something considerably more varied and dynamic than a lot of people think.

Matching and Mirroring

So how do you use your body language to create rapport? To put it simply—you mimic the other person. Or, to give the proper term, you reflect a *postural echo.* In other words, you observe the other person's posture, the angle of her head, how she holds her arms, and so on, and then do the same. If she moves some part of her body, you move the same part of your own body. There are two different ways you can do this. They are called *matching* and *mirroring,* and both are based on the same idea. Which method you choose to use really only depends on how you're standing or sitting in relation to the other person. With matching, you move the corresponding part of your body when the person you want to match moves (i.e., if she moves her right arm, you move your right arm). Matching is suitable if you're sitting or standing next to the person whose body language you're going to follow. With mirroring, you move the opposite part of your body (i.e., she moves her right arm, you move your left arm), as if you were her mirror image. Mirroring is used when you're sitting or standing opposite each other.

Obviously, if you started copying someone too closely it would look very peculiar. For one thing, it would be an obvious change in your own behavior when you shift from moving as you usually would to moving the way the person you're talking to does. And if you were to go on to mimic that person's movements exactly, it would be extremely obvious what you were up to. Instead of creating rapport, you would give the impression of being a schizophrenic lunatic. Watch the film *Single White Female* if you want an idea of what *not* to do.

When creating rapport by adapting to another person's communication, it's important to do so discreetly and gradually. To start with, make very small changes and increase them gradually at a very cautious rate. How quickly or slowly you do this is determined by the extent to which you perceive that you're getting the desired response. The more interested and involved you can make the other person feel, the more openly you can imitate her body language. This also applies once rapport has already been established.

When you adapt your own behavior to somebody else's, you need to be subtle about it and do it gradually.

To start with, you should use representative gestures (another fancy term). In other words, you mimic the other person, but only a little. As long as you're consistent in following the other person's body language, you can tone the movements down. If she crosses her arms, you can put your right hand on your left wrist. You do the same thing, but on a smaller scale. In this way, you can avoid having the other person consciously begin to wonder what you're up to.

Another good way of masking the fact that you're adjusting to somebody's behavior is to delay your movements. Instead of doing something directly after the other person has done it, you can wait for twenty or thirty seconds before you do it. As long as you're consistent, this will still be registered by the other person's unconscious mind, which will pick up the fact that the two of you have the same patterns of movement and are "alike."

A third way of concealing what you are doing is to imitate the other person's facial expressions. The other person's facial expressions are a reflection of how he's feeling inside (because our mental and physical processes are linked). If he sees a corresponding expression on your face, he will perceive that you feel the same way he does, because you look the way he does. And this makes for an extremely close connection. Because we can't see our own faces, it's practically impossible to discover that someone else is mimicking our facial expressions; we just get a feeling of affinity. Just be careful that whatever you're matching is a specific expression and not just how somebody looks naturally. Some people look sad, stern, or angry when they are actually just relaxed, depending on how their faces are constructed. Make sure you know how the person you are matching looks otherwise, so you can differentiate between his ordinary face and his genuine expressions of emotion.

Also make sure that you move at the same speed, in the same *tempo,* as the other person. This is particularly important for any gestures that are interactive, such as shaking hands. If you're dealing with a slow person, you need a slow handshake, and vice versa. If you notice that the other person talks quickly and seems wound up, you ought to increase the speed of your handshake. Other rhythmic gestures, like nodding your head when you agree, must also be adapted to the right tempo. Later in the book you'll learn how to get an idea, even at a first meeting, of the sort of tempo at which somebody else speaks or thinks.

Don't Overinterpret Things

As I wrote earlier, most of our gestures don't have universal meanings, which are the same for all people. However, there is a dictionary of sorts for most people's personal body language. We will often use the same gestures each time we're in a certain mood, even if nobody else uses that particular gesture. So try not to put too much stock into your interpretations of somebody's body language when you first meet. You should note, for instance, if her left leg moves, but avoid immediately interpreting that as a sign that she is nervous, unless there are other indications that this is the case. After a while, you will learn to associate some people's motions and poses with specific thoughts and emotions. Perhaps that left leg was a sign of nerves after all, but that principle would still only apply to her, and not necessarily reveal anything at all about somebody else. We all express ourselves in our own special ways. Once you have some skill at reading the body language of others, you will notice that you are becoming much better at anticipating what somebody is about to say, just before she says it. You will basically be reading minds!

By beginning to observe others in a new way, you'll also soon begin to notice changes in them, changes that, even though you can't imitate them, can provide a lot of information about how they feel and what they are thinking. You will readily notice things like changes in skin tone. When we are afraid, our faces often turn paler. If we blush, it doesn't have to happen to the cheeks. Blushing can also be observed at the top of the ears, or at the forehead, jawline, neck, or chest. You will notice when somebody's pupils dilate, a sign of interest and involvement. There will be more on this later on. I just want to let you know that you will soon start to notice things you previously wouldn't have believed anybody could see.

What do you do when somebody is obviously using distancing body language? Do you mimic that, too? There is no consensus on this issue. Some feel that would be a terrible idea, while others recommend it. Those who recommend it claim that since one of the reasons you establish rapport in the first place is so you can lead the other person when necessary, you ought to get into rapport by adapting to another's body language and then gradually change your own body language to open it up and make it more positive. This way, you can affect change in the other. This is a good idea, but I think you need to take the context into account. If there is tension in the air, I think you can do better than to mirror negative body language. There are so many other things you can do to get into rapport, and crossing your arms may not be the best idea. However, if there are no signs that it really is a case of negative body language (perhaps the person is just a bit cold and that is why she crossed her arms), mirroring it can make sense.

Body Language as Therapy

One of the reasons for consciously establishing rapport is, as I mentioned earlier, to allow you to lead the other person into a (desired) mental state. It works because we want to follow each other when we're in rapport. The cost of not doing so is broken rapport, and unconsciously we'd do almost anything to avoid that. When you manage to change somebody's blocking body language into a more open one, you're not just changing the body language; you're changing the person's entire attitude. Those two things are connected, remember? What happens to the body also happens to the mind.

Another very practical use is turning around negative states in friends and loved ones. This is a classic therapeutic method that you can easily use yourself. It's useful when your friend is a bit down for no particular reason. Maybe it's a rainy Monday on the last week before payday. Go ahead and mirror that person's body language! Don't express the negative emotions with your body to the same extent as your friend is doing; you don't want to drag him or her down even further. You want to do just enough to establish rapport and make it clear you understand where he or she is at. When you've checked to make sure that you're in good rapport, gradually allow your own body language to open up and become more positive. Straighten your back, open up your gestures, move your arms away from your body, and start smiling. At every step along the way, check that your friend joins you in the change. When you lose him or her and your lead is no longer being picked up, you can back up a step and regain rapport. Leading somebody, in rapport, is a case of two steps forward, one step back.

When you have achieved a sufficient change in the other's body language, you will have changed his or her mood to the same extent. The blues will be blown away. You see, it's impossible to be down if your back is straight and you keep your chin up and smile. Try it!

You just need to remember never to do this to somebody who has a real problem. A person in a state of mourning, for instance, needs to remain in it for some time. Sorrow is a state in which we conserve energy and mentally process the events that caused the emotion. If you perform this exercise with somebody who is experiencing genuine sorrow, the mental processing needed for him or her to move on will be blocked. In those cases, you're better off leaving the person in her sad, but necessary, state. But, like I said, for someone who just has the plain old blues, it's perfect!

OBSERVATION EXERCISES

1. The next time you're in a restaurant, you can observe for yourself how people who are in rapport follow and lead each other. Find a couple or a group of friends that seem to have an intimate, close, and firmly established relationship. Watch them take turns following and leading each other's body language while they speak to each other.

2. You could also try to spot people who sit the same way as whoever is next to them in the room.

3. Or try to figure out who knows each other and who doesn't on a full bus, streetcar, or subway train. Here's a clue: look for people who are sitting and moving the same way. Even if they're not right next to each other, the pattern will be obvious to you.

EXERCISES FOR SHY PEOPLE

You can do these exercises if you're a little intimdated by the idea of mimicking a person you're talking to.

1. Watch a talk show or a debate on TV. Sit in the same position and move the same way as the person being interviewed or speaking. You will notice that you know more or less what that person is going to say before he has even said it. This isn't particularly surprising. After all, he's sitting the way he is because he's thinking certain thoughts. If you follow his movements and positions, you will initiate similar mental processes and moods in yourself. Pay attention to how your emotions and your perception of yourself change as you adopt different body postures.

2. Establishing rapport from a distance. If you're in a public space or some other social environment, you can choose somebody you're not directly in contact with, somebody at the other end of the room, and begin adapting to that person's body language. Don't be too surprised if, before long, this person asks you if you know each other from somewhere. It's only to be expected that she'd find you familiar, as you're her own mirror image! So you should pick somebody you wouldn't mind talking to, not somebody you'd rather avoid. This is actually a secret method for picking up people you're too shy to actually talk to, and getting them interested in you.

3. A good way to get rid of the feeling that this person is going to "catch you out" is to make her tell you about herself. Then start mirroring her body language shamelessly while making noises of agreement, like "mm-hmm" and "yeah." Notice how she's not paying attention to anything you're doing. When we're talking about ourselves or are very angry, we shut the rest of the world out. We talk about ourselves, to ourselves, with ourselves, and seldom notice anything anybody else is doing.

When you begin establishing rapport, you may feel troubled by a feeling that the whole thing is unnatural, that it's simply not you. That's completely correct; in that case it isn't you. Not yet. The unnatural feeling is just a matter of getting into the habit. When you learned to ride a bike, the connection between making a circular pedaling motion and moving forward was completely unnatural at first. But then you learned how to do it, and eventually you reached the fourth stage of learning, and cycling became one of your internalized, unconscious skills. It became a part of you. Your practical skills at establishing rapport can become a natural part of you in the same way. All you need in order to acquire the habit is to start doing it.

How Do You Really Sound?

How to Use Your Voice

The voice is another powerful tool for establishing rapport. The same principle is at play here: you adapt your own voice to the way the other person uses hers. Of course, again, this has to happen gradually and with discretion. And just as in the case of body language, there is no need for exact and perfect imitation. The fact is, even if you could get away with imitating somebody's body language perfectly, it would still seem extremely strange if you suddenly started sounding exactly like the person you're talking to. But there's always some quality of the other person's voice that you can adapt to, some trait you can at least *approximate*. Listen and see how he or she uses the following elements of speech:

Tonality

Is it a deep or a light voice? Many men speak in a deeper voice than their larynxes are really made for, and many women speak in a lighter voice than they really ought to. This is because of cultural impact on our behavior. We believe ourselves to be emphasizing our masculinity or femininity this way.

Fullness

Is it a rich voice with a lot of different timbres, or is it thin and airy? As a result of cultural imprints, we consider full and rich voices potent, serious, and reliable, while airier voices seem feminine and seductive. An airy voice can also make a childish impression.

Melody

Is this a monotonous voice, which remains on a single tone all the time? Monotonous voices often don't use falling intonation at the end of a proposition, or rising intonation at the end of a question. This can often make it hard to understand what somebody with a monotonous voice really means—was the person asking a question or making a claim? Or was it a joke, even? The counterpoint to this would be a melodic voice, which uses many different tones in speech. Scandinavians, especially Norwegians, are famous for their melodic and songlike speech.

Tempo

Is this person speaking quickly or slowly? We speak at the same speed as we think and understand things, so if you speak slower than people you are talking to, you will bore them into thinking about something other than the message you're trying to communicate. At worst, this could cause them to get restless and start waiting for you to finish so they can wrap up the conversation before it costs them any more time. On the other hand, if you speak faster than they are used to, you run the risk of losing them, and they might not pick up the important points of what you have to say. Men are commonly thought to speak faster than women, but this is a false stereotype. Researcher Tyler Schnoebelen found that women in mixed-gender settings actually slowed down their speech tempo to allow men to be those who spoke the fastest even when they really weren't!

Strength and Volume

Adapting to somebody else's volume is a good tactic. A soft-spoken person will appreciate you quieting your voice down. Somebody who belts his words out in speech will respect you more if you raise the volume of your voice.

As you can see, a voice has many different properties for you to mirror. If you're going to choose just one thing to work with, I'd recommend you adapt your tempo. Rapport is, to a great extent, a matter of mirroring the other person's tempo, and in the case of speech it produces especially good results. Some claim that adapting your vocal tempo is the most important technique for establishing rapport. I'm not sure that's entirely true, but it is a very powerful technique. The voice is especially important, since it is sometimes the only tool we have for communication—on the phone, for instance. Zuker, whom we mentioned earlier, reports on a study performed on behalf of a telemarketing company that wanted to increase its revenues. It sold magazine subscriptions, and for this reason it was in contact with each prospective customer once, or at the most twice, before it had either failed or closed the deal. For the experiment, the sales team was divided into two groups. One group continued to work the same way they had done previously, while the other was given an extra instruction: try to pace your speech to that of the person you're calling. Using only this difference in methodology, the latter group increased its sales by almost 30 percent, while the first group made no improvement over the previous sales figures. I'll repeat that: all the latter group did was adapt the tempo of speech to the person the group was speaking to. Even if you're not in sales, a positive increase of almost 30 percent is a lot, no matter what you do and what your relationships are about, especially when all you have to do is keep track of how quickly or slowly you are speaking.

We speak at the same pace as we think and understand things. If you speak in the same tempo as the person you are talking to, your thoughts are expressed at the same pace he or she is using to think.

Idiom

Changing Your Expressions

The things we're about to discuss are not exactly wordless, but I'd still like to mention them since they offer you yet another way to get into good rapport with people. We all have preferred variations in the ways we use language. What follows are some examples of these kinds of personal touches and idioms used in language. In establishing rapport, it's always a good thing to be able to adapt to these or any other similar linguistic practices. Of course, you have to know enough about the cultural references involved to be able to adapt your communication in a believable way.

Slang

Slang is quite difficult to adapt to, as it is specific to trends, geographical locations, and age groups. It is always changing, and an expression that's awesome today could be lame tomorrow. If you feel like you're savvy enough to mirror a certain kind of slang used by the person you want to be in rapport with, go for it! But if you don't know how to respond to "Wassup bro?" you're better off not trying. There is a lot of potential for embarrassment here. Slang also functions as a way of signaling that you belong to a certain group, an age group, for instance, so you also have to consider how likely you are to be taken seriously when representing yourself as a member of the group in question. If you come across a slang expression that signals an age group, and you're the wrong age to use it, you can show that you're hip enough to know the meaning of the word and respond to it, but that doesn't mean you should use it yourself unless you're "entitled" to it, that is to say, unless you could plausibly be seen as belonging to the group of people who share that particular slang usage.

Jargon

In many conversations, expressions are used that are only needed for the specific topic of discussion. When you're talking about boats, boating terms are likely to be used. By using jargon *to the same extent* as the person you're talking to, you're showing him or her that you have the same understanding and knowledge of the topic. This goes both ways. If somebody uses more technical terms than you would normally, but you have the knowledge to adapt to the speech of the other, go ahead. If somebody uses fewer technical terms than you would normally, hold back on your own use of them. For example, if someone points at a screen or monitor and says, "The computer is broken," there's probably no point in asking him how many partitions he has on his C: drive. Ask him if he's pressed the green ON button.

Personal Experiences

Despite having spent a lot of time in school, very few people speak the way a grammar textbook tells you to. We tend to add superfluous, unnecessary words, like, all over the place, especially, you know, at the end of a sentence and stuff. Or begin sentences with dependent clauses. If you hear somebody use expressions like this, do the same thing!

Trance Words

We all have favorite words. Words we use a lot, in all kinds of situations. They could be slang expressions, bits of jargon, or something completely different. Often they'll be something we've picked up from someone else and made a habit of saying. We occasionally become painfully aware of these words. When we catch ourselves using one of them, we might burst out: "GAAAHH! I have to stop saying 'awesome'!" But we have a lot of other favorite words that we don't always notice in this way. These words personalize our use of language and make it slightly different from everyone else's. Milton H. Erickson, the biggest name in modern hypnotherapy, called these personal words "trance words," as in hypnotic trance. A very fast way of getting into rapport with somebody is to pay attention to her trance words, that is, words she often uses when speaking, and then use those words yourself. You begin speaking her language, showing her you're just like her, and you will be clearly understood since you even use the same words when you speak.

I understand if you're starting to feel that I'm asking too much of you. How are you supposed to listen to how somebody else is using her voice, adapt your own voice to it, while discovering and following her personal language usage—preferably including an analysis of her syntax—and remember what you were going to say? Believe me, it's not as difficult as it sounds. Just as you already adapt your body language somewhat to others, you already do a lot of these things.

Let me give you a mundane example of mind reading: I know that at some time, you ended a phone conversation, and the other people in the room with you knew who you'd been talking to without you having mentioned any names or given them any other clues during the conversation. When you asked them how they knew, they said they could *hear* it from the way you spoke. Sound familiar? I thought so. They could tell who you were talking to because you *sounded like the person on the other end,* that is to say, you adapted your voice and language to sound more like the person you were talking to. It was most likely somebody close to you, who you are in good rapport with. Remember, we want acceptance and respect. We want social interaction. *We want rapport.*

Breathe, Damn You, Breathe!

Rapport by Breathing

A basic method for effective rapport is to adapt your breathing to somebody else's. The thing most writers and instructors who teach this forget to mention is how insanely difficult it usually is to see somebody breathe. Even after extensive training, seeing how somebody is breathing can be almost impossible. (I am not telling you not to bother; on the contrary, if you suddenly notice somebody's breathing, you could by all means adapt to his breathing pattern.)

Breathing is visible in different ways depending on *how* the person is breathing: heavily or lightly, with the chest or with the diaphragm. You should keep an eye on the person's stomach, chest, shoulders, and neck. Sometimes, you can find somebody's breathing rhythm by observing the movement of the shadow of his shoulders. You should also listen to the person's speech. We don't speak while inhaling, so by noticing where he pauses in his speech, you can tell when he is breathing in.

The point of trying to follow somebody's breathing, that is, to breathe at the same speed and with the same intensity, is this: when you're breathing along with somebody, you are entering the same *bodily tempo* as the other person. This means that a lot of the things you would otherwise need to pay attention to for rapport purposes come naturally to you. When you change the tempo of your breathing, your body language and speech will follow automatically. It will also make it easier for you to find a matching voice level.

If you can synchronize your breathing completely with that of another person, the connection between you can feel magical. Unfortunately, it's far from easy to do. Physical differences can sometimes even make it impossible to breathe exactly the same as somebody else. My ex-wife is about five feet two inches tall, and weighed 104 pounds when we were married. I am five feet nine inches and weigh 163 pounds. On top of this, she breathed with her chest, which meant she inhaled less air than her lung capacity would have allowed. I couldn't follow her breathing for more than a minute before losing my breath. Of course, you're not supposed to be asphyxiating yourself by trying to follow somebody's breathing. But try to get your breathing as close as you can without struggling.

As I said earlier, use your knowledge about the other person's tempo for all rhythmic actions, like nods or handshakes, so these motions will also be paced correctly and won't break your rapport.

At first, you'll get good mileage out of trying to observe the person's *general tempo* rather than trying to follow his or her breathing exactly, and then beginning to breathe at that tempo without worrying about following each and every breath. It's quite possible you will begin to follow the person's breathing exactly after a while, but even if you don't, you will have achieved the most important thing: synchronizing your general tempo.

Noticing somebody's breathing and trying to breathe the same way is also a quick way to understand the mood somebody is in. This kind of knowledge is useful in situations where you feel like you're in rapport but that something is disturbing your relationship.

Start following the other person's breathing. If you notice that the person is breathing fast and high up in the chest, even though she seems calm and safe, you can tell that there is most likely some concern she is trying to hide from you. This kind of information is priceless in a lot of situations. The best thing is that you don't need to remember which moods belong with which type of breathing. By simply breathing the way the other person is, you will feel the mood, in this case anxiety, *yourself,* and so you'll know exactly what emotional state she is in.

CUDDLE EXERCISE

If you know somebody you can cuddle without having to explain that it is part of a rapport-making exercise—maybe your partner at home—you should cuddle that person in a way that makes his or her breathing very clear to you. Begin by noticing the vast difference between breathing in sync and breathing out of sync with each other. Follow the other's breathing for a minute or so. Then carefully change the pace of your own breathing. If the other person follows your change unconsciously, you have established rapport by using your breathing.

Hypnosis experts Martin Nyrup and Ian Harling suggest trying this without any clothes on. If you are lucky enough to have somebody you can cuddle with in the nude (I recommend it be somebody you know), at sleep time, for instance, you should try breathing in and out of sync in those conditions. You will sense a very clear and tangible difference between, on the one hand, total connectedness, and on the other hand, an uncomfortable sense of being alienated from the person who is close to you.

The Energizer Bunny vs. Garfield, the Cat

Pay Attention to Energy Levels

Let's zoom out a little and get a more holistic view of the person you are trying to get into rapport with. Of course, you need to be able to notice where this person is in terms of emotional state and energy levels. Later on in this book, I will teach you to identify different emotional states in a lot more detail than is possible based purely on breathing. The best way to determine somebody's energy levels, however, is to observe his posture and breathing, and use your *prior knowledge of the person in question.*

Some people are a little withdrawn before lunchtime. They get to work in the morning, mumble something resembling "g'mornin'," and sink into their chairs. They are wearing invisible "do not disturb" signs until eleven or so, and it's not until after lunch, or their fifth cup of coffee, that they actually open their eyes and crawl out of their shells. This doesn't mean their work is any less good. It just means the social aspects of their beings need longer to kick into gear. These people rarely have particularly fast bodily tempos, even after five cups of coffee (all that does is make them jittery). They're like Garfield, the cat. We're all in that mood from time to time, but for some of us it is more of a permanent state.

Then, of course, we have their opposites: the people who are always full of energy, perseverance, and determination. They run six miles to work each morning, swoop into the office with a big smile, half an hour before everybody else shows up, and almost never miss their lunchtime workouts. And at the end of the day, they run all the way back home.

I once had a colleague who was like that. He was, or rather *is,* a father of seven. That hour he spent alone at the office every day—after he had run or cycled to work—was spent on editing his home videos from the weekend, including DVD menus and extra audio tracks. He's nothing like Garfield; he's more of an Energizer Bunny type.

Garfield and the Energizer Bunny can have a hard time getting along.

You might be one of those people who shows up at work bursting with energy. If you encounter a sleepy and introverted colleague, whose approval you happen to be in desperate need of for a project, it might be a good idea to tone yourself down a bit. Try not to be enthusiastic enough for both of you, at least at first. If you turn up with a loud cheer, fresh from the gym, spilling protein powder all over his laptop, you're almost guaranteed a no. It goes the other way, too. If you're one of those slow, cautious people, you could probably use a way to fire yourself up. It's likely that your lethargy is a little annoying to the more energetic people around you. Fortunately, there is an easy way to fix this.

ENERGY EXERCISE

Do you remember how you used body language to make positive change happen for your friend when she was down? It worked because our physical and mental states are connected. You can use the same principle to change you own mood or energy level. You simply start acting *as if* you were more energetic or happy. Imagine the face you would have, and how you would be sitting, standing, or moving your body if you had a lot more energy than you do right now. At first you may feel a little strange, but you'll soon notice that you actually *are* more energetic and positive than just before. Let the bodily reactions that you can control, what you're doing with your muscles and motion, activate processes in your brain. Fake it 'til you make it, basically.

Or, as the famous psychologist William James put it already in 1922, in this proto self-help book *On Vital Reserves: The Energies of Men, The Gospel of Relaxation*: "Action seems to follow feeling, but really action and feeling go together; and by regulating the action, which is under the more direct control of the will, we can indirectly regulate the feeling, which is not."

So the best way to make yourself happy when you're not is to sit as if you hadn't a care in the world, look around with a happy face, and act and talk as if you were happy!

Energy levels are not very difficult to figure out. It's more a matter of common sense than detailed analysis for adaptation of your communication tools, even though the results will be the same, of course. Remember what I've taught you about observation, following and establishing rapport. Is eight o'clock in the morning really the right time to show somebody your wonderful report full of good ideas? Could you schedule the meeting for after lunch, when you know the other person will be more receptive? If that won't work, you have to take care to present yourself in a way that matches well with the way the other person is feeling. If you don't, you could face stiff resistance. Not because your ideas aren't good, but because your energy levels are not well matched with the person you're talking to.

Say It Like You Mean It

Be Consistent in Your Words and Actions

When we communicate with somebody, we cause different emotional states in that person, whether we want to or not. It can be done intentionally, like when we tell somebody something to make the person happy or angry or surprised. Expressions we want an emotional response to could be the following:

"Did you hear what happened?"

"I can't stand Adam Sandler!"

"I love you."

Causing emotional states can also be done unintentionally, like when what we say starts off a chain of emotional associations in the person we're talking to, without our even knowing it. "How's it going?" is something we often say with no purpose beyond acknowledging the other person. But if things are bad enough, even an innocent question like that can cause somebody to burst into tears.

We also change people's emotional states by displaying, and hence projecting, our own emotions. If we're happy, people around us tend to be in good cheer. If we're down, so are they, even when we don't say anything. Often we'll even ask people explicitly to enter different emotional states:

"Cheer up!"

"Calm down!"

To make them understand what we mean, and to seem credible, we have to project the emotion we're asking for while we say these kinds of things. If you want to calm somebody down, the wrong way to do it is to grab his shoulders, shake him about, and scream "CALMDOWNDAMMIT!!!" into his face. If you want to make somebody relax, you need to be relaxed. As a parent, I am well aware of how incredibly difficult this can be at times. But it is important nonetheless. To get the person you're talking to into the emotional state you're asking for, you have to exemplify it and show what you mean. You're better off yawning while you ask, "Are you tired, too?" than saying it while you're doing your exercise routine, at least if you want to provoke tiredness.

If you want to calm somebody down, you have to radiate calmness yourself. Don't speak too loudly, avoid fidgeting, and make sure you're breathing deeply, not at the top of your chest. If you want somebody to feel confident, you can't just talk about being confident, you have to act like you are confident. By doing this, you're also making a very clear *suggestion,* that is, a proposition or instruction given to start processes in the unconscious mind of the other person (there will be more about this clever stuff later on). It's not just about showing what you mean; you make the person understand what you're talking about in a direct, emotional way, and you show him that it's not such a big deal to get there. By establishing emotional understanding, you also create an intimate and personal experience of the same feeling in the person you're communicating with. Talking about something means relating to it on an external and analytical level, but understanding it emotionally is an internal, personal experience. Internal experiences are always the strongest. Just think of the difference between talking about a loving hug as opposed to getting one. Which would you prefer?

If there is a disconnect between the words spoken and what is communicated by body language and tone of voice, the wordless message will take priority. If somebody shouts at you to calm down, two different emotional states are communicated: the external one (the words) and the internal one (the experience). Which one will you follow? Does a situation like this make you relax, or wind you up? You don't need to be an expert mind reader to realize that the latter is the right answer.

Opinion Aikido

The Noble Art of Agreeing with People

Another powerful tool for making rapport is to *agree*. I know, it sounds like something a pushover would do. But I mean it. Here's how to do it: try to find *some* attitude or opinion held by the other person that you are prepared to agree with. This is extra important if you are also intending to try to get this person to change his or her mind about something later on. If you're looking to inform others about how things really are, you risk running into resistance if you tell the other person she is wrong. She'll enter defense mode instead of listening. The worst thing you can do if you want to convince somebody to adopt your opinions is to confront her directly. Rapport is all about making the person you're communicating with realize that you understand her, that you're just like her. That goes for opinions, too.

Of course, you shouldn't do this to the extent that you have to betray your own values and principles. However, there is usually something you can agree on. If you encounter somebody in a negotiation wherein your positions are diametrically opposed, perhaps at least you both like boats. Or *The Witcher 3*. Even if you think the other person has completely misunderstood the issue being discussed or is simply out of his mind, you can still always agree that *if you were in his position* (that is, if you had misunderstood everything, too, but of course you never say this) *you would feel the same as he does*. Even if you're dealing with a real crook, it's still true to agree that *I would do the same thing if I were you.* The simple words "If I were you, I would react in exactly the same way" can work wonders for your rapport. If you think about it, it's really obvious that if you were the other person, you would do what he's doing. But that's not how it is received; rather, we take it as evidence that somebody understands us.

Finding something to agree to, and starting from that, is the same kind of principle as you would use in the martial art of aikido. If you try to get in the way of the other person's opinions by saying, "You're wrong," you'll only start a mental wrestling match that will end up being exhausting and unproductive for both of you. Instead of getting in the way, when you say, "I feel the same way you do," you stand next to her. The energy from the other person, which you would have spent all your efforts on containing, can now be used to propel you both toward a different destination. You adopt the role of a follower rather than presenting an obstacle. The person you're talking to won't mind at all, since you're now suddenly working together to reach a common goal instead of struggling to determine who is right. You're in rapport. You are in the same place and share the same understanding. Aikido is all about not getting in the way of your opponent's momentum, and instead using it to topple your opponent if necessary.

Shakespeare for President

To a great extent, maybe entirely, our reality is constituted by our ideas of what is true. To manipulate somebody's beliefs is, therefore, to influence that person's reality. Skilled politicians have been aware of this for a long time. When you're in the opposition, it's always best to begin by agreeing with the more popular opinion before formulating the changes for the better that you would like to add. In Shakespeare's play *Julius Caesar,* Brutus, the man who had been closest to the Roman dictator, is accused of murdering Caesar, a crime he is guilty of. *"Et tu, Brute?"* But at Caesar's funeral, Brutus gives a passionate speech that convinces the people he has actually done a good deed. No matter how much Brutus loved Caesar, he realized that Caesar's deluded leadership was leading them all to ruin. Despite understanding the consequences for him personally, he decided this was the only solution. His heinous crime was motivated by his love for Rome, not by any hate for Caesar.

You simply have to love a guy like that, so the people are prepared to forgive him. However, Mark Antony is waiting in the wings and also has a speech prepared for the funeral. He wants to get Brutus convicted of murder, so he chooses to speak last, giving him the opportunity to hear what Brutus has to say first. When Antony's turn comes, he begins his speech with a surprising statement: he agrees with everybody, praising Brutus as a man of honor. Once Antony has made it clear to everybody that he agrees with them, the stage is set for his rhetoric. During the speech, he uses clever emotional arguments to make the listeners conclude that the murder was unjustified and that the murderer should be banished. If he'd started off by saying that—his actual opinion on the matter—nobody would have listened to him. So instead of getting in the way and being an obstacle, he begins by agreeing, in order to be able to take on the role of a follower. Mark Antony must have held a black belt in opinion aikido. And with rhetorical skills of that level, Shakespeare, who wrote the whole thing, should have entered politics.

First Agree, Then Lead

In summary: you shouldn't betray your own values and principles when you use opinion aikido. You shouldn't have to lie, either. All rapport has to be based on sincerity. Sometimes, finding common opinions or values is no problem, but there are situations in which it can be a lot more difficult. In negotiations and debates, the different parties are assumed to hold opposing opinions.

If you're too opposed to the issue under discussion or negotiation, it can be a good idea to find another issue for which you might have some common ground. If you can't find any common values at all, which could happen if you're having an argument with somebody in a tinfoil hat, you can always say, *"If I were you, I'd feel exactly the same as you do. I would be upset about the radio transmissions they were sending to my teeth, as well."* Naturally, this is always true. If you were the other person, of course, you would feel the same way.

If somebody storms into the room with a cloud of anger about her head, slams her fist down on the table, and shouts, "This is UNACCEPTABLE!!" the best thing for you to do is get up, put whatever you're doing down with a loud bang, and loudly state, "I AGREE!! I understand COMPLETELY why you think it's unacceptable! If I were you, I'd think it was too!" That is, use opinion aikido, while matching her body language, tone of voice, and energy level. Then, after lowering the volume and tempo of your voice a little, and perhaps even sitting down on the edge of the table, you continue: "But do you know what? I think there's a way we can solve this." You start leading, both toward a more suitable emotional state and toward the new approach or idea you have that you know might change her idea of the situation. Apart from setting a solid foundation for solving the problem together, this is a great way to extinguish the fire in people with quick tempers. A person who is angry is looking for opposition, a struggle, and wants you to get in her way so she can direct her anger at you. By affirming her anger, claiming she is entitled to be upset, and agreeing with her, you can quickly subdue her anger.

Your goal, as is always the case with rapport, is to make the other person realize you understand her. That you feel the same and are the same as her. This way, she'll also be much more willing to listen to your suggestions. If you seem to be in the same place, the other person will make more of an effort to see the value of your ideas, since that's a way to stay in rapport. *If I were you, I would feel exactly the same.* There's nothing to it.

Opinion Kung Fu: Crouching "and," Hidden "but" Style

Connecting Different Propositions

A simple technique for seemingly agreeing and making people go along with possibly dubious argumentation is to use the word "and" instead of "but." The word "but" signals reservation, while "and" ties phrases and propositions together. The linking function of "and" is so strong that it makes no difference if the two propositions being connected actually contradict each other. Good politicians have learned how to use "and" linkages. Compare these two situations, where Swift, the politician, begins by scoring some quick points by talking about something everybody considers important:

Situation 1

SWIFT: "We want to improve health care, so we have to raise taxes."
GULLIVER: "We want to improve health care, too, *but* we want to lower taxes."

Situation 2

SWIFT: "We want to improve health care, so we have to raise taxes."
GULLIVER: "I agree with you that we need to improve health care, *and* that's why we want to lower taxes."

In the first debate, Gulliver positions herself on the other side of the fence by using the word "but," which means she is contradicting Swift. By doing this, Gulliver is losing a lot of votes. In the second debate, Gulliver will score the same easy points as Swift, despite not having changed her message, and despite it still being the opposite of Swift's! "And" gives any proposition an almost causal quality, where what follows after the "and" is perceived as a near unavoidable consequence of whatever precedes it. The reservation expressed by "but" has the opposite effect.

How to Make Pen Pals

Rapport by Email

The same principles you would use in a personal meeting or a phone call will apply for written communications, which are ever more important in people's lives thanks to new technologies used in emails, text messages, and chats. Despite what you might think, you can try to follow someone's "tone of speech" even in writing. Is the person on the other end serious or lighthearted? Is she writing long sentences or short ones? Using formal language or informal? Several short paragraphs or one long one? What about personal language usages, like jargon or foreign expressions? Can you identify any trance words? How about hidden opinions? Find the form of expression the other person is using, and adapt to it as much as you can.

If you get this mail:

hey . . . checking for friday . . . still going to happen? /sa

you shouldn't answer like this:

Hi Samus!

I have investigated the matter, and concluded the most effective solution would be to schedule the meeting for the afternoon instead. Please get back to me, at your convenience, to confirm whether or not that would suit your current schedule.

Best Regards,

Henrik Fexeus

A more appropriate response would be:

hey there—friday pm ok instead?

hf

This is especially important in cases of email communication. Email has not, as people once anticipated, replaced the written letter. At least not in terms of how we use it to communicate. Email has rather replaced the telephone call. When we send emails, we express ourselves in ways that are very close to the ways we speak. The problem is that speech is entirely dependent on our use of our voice and face (or even body) to make proper sense. We need tone of voice, tempo, raised or lowered intonation at the end of sentences, emphasis using our eyebrows, head motions, and so on to really be able to decode what is said to us. (There will be more about using facial expressions to emphasize words later on.) But in email, none of these things are available. We use the words the same way we do when we speak, but without the framework to properly understand them. This is why emojis were invented, as well as strange acronyms, like lol, imho, brb (in case you don't know, they mean "laugh out loud," "in my humble opinion," and "be right back," respectively), and so on, to make sure people won't take a joke seriously or think we're trying to show off. Using the same words, phrases, and descriptions as the other person becomes vital, as it's not only a way of establishing rapport, but also creates some level of understanding.

An Old Shortcut

Getting People to Talk About Themselves

The fact that the thing everybody wants to talk about the most is themselves is an old nugget of wisdom. Early master of rapport Dale Carnegie wrote as early as 1936 that if you want people to think you're a great conversation partner, all you need to do is get them to talk about themselves. After that, you can simply sit there, nodding and making an occasional encouraging noise!

Getting somebody to talk about herself is, naturally, also a good way of getting her into a state where she isn't consciously paying attention to what you're doing, as mentioned earlier. It's a good idea for occasions when you'd like to practice matching body language. But most of all, getting people to talk about themselves is a quick shortcut to good rapport.

Putting It to the Test

Making Sure You're in Rapport

There are several different ways of making sure you're in rapport with somebody. One of the reasons for establishing rapport is to make you able to lead the other, so why not begin by checking if you can do that? Make a change in your body language or speech tempo, and see if the other person follows you. If she's following you, she'll make the same change herself. When you're in good rapport, you take turns leading and following each other. If the person you're establishing rapport with doesn't follow when you try to lead, you go back to following and reestablish the relationship. Then wait for a new opportunity to start leading. Most interactions involve constant following and leading, back and forth, until both parties are agreed or the conversation is over.

Where Is the Other Person's Focus?

Noticing where the other person is focusing her attention is a good thing to do if you want to make sure you have her interest. You want her to be sitting comfortably, preferably with both feet on the floor or with one leg crossed over the other, so that it's clear she's not about to head off somewhere. If you are standing up, the

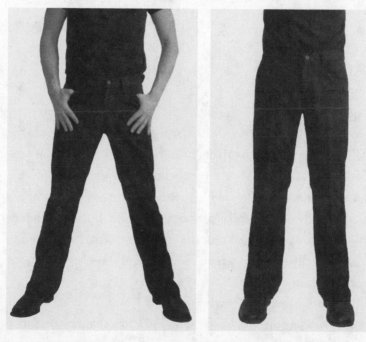

CONFIDENT   NEUTRAL

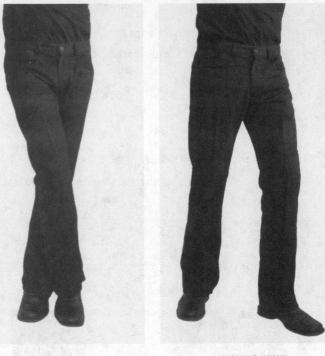

INFERIOR   MOVING AWAY

other person's feet should be pointed straight at you. A macho pose, most commonly used by men, with the legs spread wide and maybe even thumbs planted in the pants pockets, reveals a confident attitude. Somebody whose legs are parallel to each other is adopting a neutral attitude to you. Crossed legs either mean the person needs to go to the bathroom or feels inferior to you. All of these different leg positions, however, mean that the person is prepared to listen to you. The only difference is where the owner of those legs positions him- or herself in the social ladder compared to you.

On the other hand, a "cowboy position," with one leg slightly bent and the foot pointing to the side, indicates that the person is already moving away from you in his mind.

The last picture is a frozen tai chi moment. This person has started shifting his weight to one leg, started to move, and is frozen midway. Don't get that confused with simply standing with one leg in front of the other. We often do that, but keep our center of gravity back. In this case, the center of gravity has moved forward. He is standing still at the moment, but once the motion is finished, the center of gravity will be moved across the leg, the leg will stretch, and he'll be walking away. This doesn't necessarily mean that this person has grown tired of your company, even though it *could* mean that. It just means that somewhere in his mind, he's started to consider what to do next. Maybe he has an appointment to keep, or has noticed somebody else he should talk to while he has the opportunity, and so on. No matter how much this person wants to continue listening to you, you no longer have his undivided attention, so you might as well do him a favor and finish the conversation as soon as you can. Whatever you do, don't try to make some final, important points as you end the conversation. Chances are he won't remember them anyway. If you still have important things left to say, you're better off saving them for the next time you meet, so you should finish things quickly and make an appointment to meet again.

To be absolutely sure his focus is on you, you would also like the person to be looking you in the eyes as you speak, and not looking past you, looking at your ears, or scanning the room for emergency exits (both physical and psychological). If you are seated, an interested person will also lean toward you slightly.

Observe the Pupils

You can also observe the size of people's pupils. It may seem difficult to keep track of things like this, but it's easier than you think. When something interests us, our pupils dilate. In a study, body-language experts Patryk and Kasia Wezowski found that this dilation is 5–15 percent, which makes it far too subtle to allow you to discern whether someone's pupils are larger or smaller than usual, but still obvious enough that the actual *change itself,* the movement when the pupil dilates or contracts, will be clearly noticeable. What you're looking for, therefore, are *changes* in pupil size. Of course, the pupils are also affected by things like light and dark. In dark rooms, we need more light to be able to see, so our pupils open wider. The fact is that all it takes for somebody's pupils to expand is for you to be wearing dark clothes when you're talking to him or her. So large pupils do not necessary mean that you have rapport or that somebody is interested in you. It might just be a reaction to the lighting, or an indication that the person is as high as a kite, for instance. So what you're actually looking for are changes. If you see someone's pupils dilate while the environmental conditions (like lighting) remain the same, it's a sign that he or she has become more interested and involved in what you're talking about.

I don't know if it's true or not, but there are loads of books that describe how jade merchants in ancient China started to wear spectacles darkened with soot to conceal their pupils. Tradition demanded bargaining and haggling over the price when one bought gemstones, and if the buyer was seen to be particularly interested in a certain piece of jade, the price would obviously go up.

PUPIL EXERCISE

Start talking to someone about something terribly boring, like the fact that the copy machine at your office is broken. Note the size of the person' pupils at this point. This is the neutral size, which is caused by lighting conditions. Now change the subject and talk about something you know interests this person a lot: her children or her boat, for example. Notice the obvious dilation of the pupils, which occurs as she becomes more interested in the conversation. It's just like watching a camera lens open up.

So people tried to control their behavior as much as they could, but the one thing that always betrayed the buyer's interest was the size of his pupils. More recently, poker players have discovered the same trick. The next time you see one of the big championships on TV, see how many of the players in the final are wearing dark glasses. Other popular accessories are scarves and hats. No matter how good your poker face is, you still can't control your autonomous nervous system. Whether you like it or not, your pupils will react—along with other things, like your pulse and sweating—when you get worked up or excited.

An interested person has dilated pupils, and someone who shows an interest in you is someone that you will in turn be interested in. It goes without saying that we like people who like us, doesn't it? In this context, changes in pupil size are extremely powerful signals that our unconscious minds react to in a big way. In a famous experiment by psychologist Eckhard Hess, men were shown identical pictures of a woman's face, the only difference being that her pupils had been enlarged in one of the pictures. These two pictures were shown to a group of heterosexual men, who were then asked which picture they found most attractive. The picture with the larger pupils was consistently thought to show a more attractive person than the unmanipulated picture—in spite of the fact that the test subjects were unable to explain why they thought so, since they couldn't see any difference between the pictures. At least not consciously. But the woman in one of the pictures had larger pupils, which signaled a greater interest in the man who was looking at her than her clone in the other picture. And this made her more attractive in the eyes of the test subjects.

Beauty is definitely in the eye of the beholder—and in how great we imagine our chances to be.

When Won't It Work?

Situations in Which You Shouldn't Follow Somebody's Behavior

Naturally, there are some situations in which you *shouldn't* adapt to somebody's behavior. I would urge you not to follow things you think the person might find bothersome or unsatisfactory about herself, like a limp or other handicap. You also shouldn't mirror somebody's stutter or asthmatic breathing. A lot of people with strong dialects are very aware of this fact, especially if they have moved away from the region where it is spoken. Being a little ashamed of your dialect is not at all unusual, especially in larger urban areas. For this reason, you should avoid speaking in dialect if you don't otherwise do so. Generally, you should avoid any kind of tics or other nervous behaviors. And as I said earlier, you shouldn't agree with things you don't really agree with. Don't ignore your own feelings. There's usually plenty of other stuff you're more pre-pared to agree with. When somebody is experiencing strong nega-tive emotions, like anger or sadness, you should avoid getting as angry or sad as he or she is. But you should feel free to adapt your own commitment and energy levels to help you better understand the situation and what the person is going through, and to help you establish rapport.

The master hypnotist Milton H. Erickson said something clever, which works just as well for situations in which you want rapport as it does for life in general: whenever you do something, if you notice that it doesn't work, stop whatever it is that you are doing and do something else. If you don't get any results by following somebody's body language, you should do something else. Start following her voice or her opinions. Or follow her actual thought patterns (we'll discuss how in the next chapter).

The tools you have been given now are more than sufficient for establishing good rapport, but they all hinge on you following somebody else's behavior, without knowing what caused it. So far, we have been content to observe other people from the outside. In the next chapter, we'll make our way inside their minds, to understand what other people are actually thinking and how to tell.

Whenever you do something, if you notice that it doesn't work, stop whatever it is that you are doing and do something else.—MILTON H. ERICKSON

If you think about different situations in your life in which you made no progress, you will probably realize that the reason you got stuck in the first place was that you were stubbornly attempting the same failed solution over and over again. The simplest solutions are often the hardest to find.

4

Senses and Thinking

HOW OUR THOUGHTS ARE DETERMINED BY OUR SENSORY IMPRESSIONS

In which you will get to eat a lemon, take a walk on the beach, and find an understanding for how our sensory impressions determine our thoughts and our behaviors.

So far, you have learned about how our thoughts, feelings, and mental states affect us physically, and that the opposite also holds. At this point, we'll have to go back to the beginning, the very beginning, for the truth is, we started somewhere in the middle. If you're going to learn to read thoughts, I think we should spend a little time discussing what thoughts really are. But don't worry; this isn't a theoretical or strictly academic matter. It is, just like everything else in this book, something you will definitely be able to use in practice.

When we think, we generally initiate one of two different processes. Either we remember, that is, we repeat thoughts we've had before, or we construct new thoughts that we haven't had before. Either way, our sensory impressions play an important part in our thinking. Our senses of hearing, vision, feeling, taste, smell, and balance are not only important for navigating our environment but are also used when we think about things that are not related to the direct sensory input we receive. We use our *memories of different sensory impressions and experiences* to think. If we reflect on a memory, like a vacation we enjoyed, we do it by visualizing what it looked like, imagining the sounds we heard there, perhaps even the smells, and so on. When we remember, we re-create sensory impressions we have had previously. However, sensory impressions are also important for constructing new thoughts. The following text is inspired by a classic hypnotic induction, in which the technique of getting the subject to internalize his or her thought processes is used. Read the text and try to immerse yourself in it as much as you can (and don't worry—you won't get hypnotized!):

Imagine walking on a beach. You're barefoot, and you can feel the sand yield to your feet as you walk. It is evening time, so the sand is nice and cool between your toes. The sun is low in the sky, and you have to squint when you face it. The only sound you can hear is that of the waves rolling in and out and an occasional seagull shrieking as it swoops over the water. You stop for a moment and take a deep breath. You can smell the seaweed in the air. You see a shell in the sand and pick it up. You hold the shell in your hand, touching its coarse and white surface with your thumb. You put the shell in your pocket and start walking again. Now you begin to hear voices murmur, and laughter, and in the light ahead you can see the silhouettes of people sitting in an outdoor restaurant. You start to smell the scent of the food and realize how hungry you are. Your mouth begins to water, and you pick up your pace as the scents and noises grow stronger.

If you were truly immersed in that story, you could practically hear the waves beating, feel the sand between your toes, and smell the seaweed. Your mouth may even have watered at the end. All this despite the fact that you may never have had an experience exactly like the one I described. If you couldn't remember the experience, it had to be constructed. To understand the story, you made a jigsaw puzzle from pieces of other, similar memories. You have held a seashell, so you know what that feels like. You know the smell of seaweed. But perhaps you've never walked on a beach at sunset and have no such memory available to use, so you created it from images you've seen, other people's stories, movie scenes, and other impressions that helped you re-create the experience. In a way, you created a new experience in your mind, which became just as real as if you'd actually experienced it.

We're always using our sensory impressions in this way when we think. Sometimes we do it in our minds, internally, as you did when you wandered through that story just now. On other occasions, we use our sensory impressions externally, as we do when we perceive the world around us. We are continuously switching between using our senses internally (in our minds) and externally (when we experience our surroundings). The more we concentrate on what somebody is saying to us, or the contents of a text we're reading, the more internal we become. For instance, you have no idea right now how your left big toe feels. That is, until you were just reminded of it, and automatically zoomed out, externally, to make sure. Big toe? I remember, I have one of those!

Our brain doesn't distinguish very well between internal and external use of our senses, and more or less the same areas of the brain are activated in both cases.

SOUR EXERCISE OR: A CHEAP HALLUCINATION

Imagine holding a peeled lemon. Feel its weight and softness in your hand. It's a little sticky from all the juice. You can smell the strong scent of the juice. And now imagine taking a good bite out of the lemon. Imagine the sour lemon juice filling your mouth and dripping down your throat.

If you really imagined that, you will have had a physical reaction: your mouth will have contracted, and your saliva production will have increased. And all you did was use your imagination and an internal sensory impression. Your brain reacted, sending the same signals to your body (your mouth, in this case) as it would have done if the sensory impression had been external, i.e., if you'd really bitten into a lemon.

Here's an interesting question to ponder: If our brains have such a hard time separating imaginary situations from actual experiences of the world, how are we to know what is real and what is a hallucination? And is there any real difference? That's worth thinking about.

Sensory Impressions

We Prefer Different Kinds of Sensory Impressions

Our sensory impressions are an important part of the content of our thoughts. We also prefer certain sensory impressions to others. Which ones we prefer varies for different people, but a large number of people prefer visual impressions for (internally) thinking about or (externally) experiencing the world. Others prefer auditory input. A third group prefers kinesthetic impressions, i.e., all physical impressions, like touch, temperature, and so on. The internal elements that correspond to kinesthetic sensory impressions are our emotions. Very emotional people belong to this group. ("How do you feel?" can be about your emotional state just as readily as it can be about a sprained ankle.) A small number of people prefer taste and smell input. For practical purposes, they are often grouped with the kinesthetics, however.

Finally, there is a group of people that don't prefer any of the mentioned sensory impressions when they reason about the world. They use logical deduction and principles and like to deliberate carefully, even debating with themselves. They are often called digital or binary thinkers, since to them everything is either right or wrong, yes or no, black or white. There is rarely any middle ground here. I refer to them as neutral, as they are not as dependent on external stimuli as the visual, auditory, or kinesthetic groups.

Of course, we all use all of these sensory impressions, but to greater or lesser extents. One of our senses is dominant, and we use it the most. The others are used to verify that whatever information our dominant, or primary, sense has given us is correct. We also vary in how we prioritize our senses and what weight we give them. Some people are extremely visual, for instance. They rely almost entirely on their visual experiences and hardly use their other senses at all. Others are mainly auditory, but use their visual impressions almost as much. Others still are mainly visual, but use memories—first emotional ones and auditory ones second—to support and verify their visual experiences. And so on.

Different Senses Make for Different
Ways of Thinking

This is an interesting thing to know. Depending on which sensory impression we prefer, we understand the world in a certain way, which can differ from the way others understand the world. We find different things important and communicate in different ways, depending on which sensory impressions we use to interpret the world around us. If you know of an easy way to find out what sensory impressions somebody prefers, you will also, to a great extent, be able to understand how she thinks, how she prefers to communicate, and what is important or uninteresting to her. Having this kind of knowledge about other people will improve your mind-reading skills immensely, not to mention your rapport skills. Now I'll give you that easy way.

Looking Around

Eye Movements and Sensory Impressions

In neuroscience, it has been known for some time that when we think, we activate different parts of the brain, and depending on which part is being activated, our eyes seem to move in certain ways. This connection has been named LEM, or lateral eye movement. In the late seventies, psychology student Richard Bandler and linguist John Grinder, the founders of the often controversial field of Neuro-Linguistic Programming, formulated a theory of something they called EAC—eye accessing cues. They had already understood that sensory impressions were very important to our thought processes, and now they claimed that you can tell which sensory impressions are activated by observing eye movements. The EAC model looks like this:

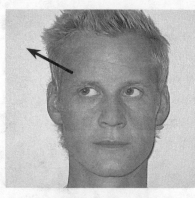

CONSTRUCTING IMAGE

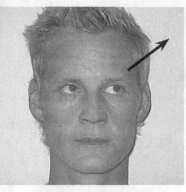

REMEMBERING IMAGE

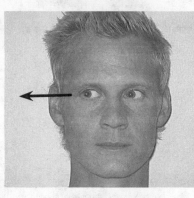

CONSTRUCTING SOUND

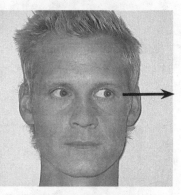

REMEMBERING SOUND

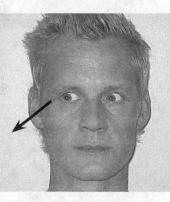

FEELING AND TOUCH (KINESTHETIC)

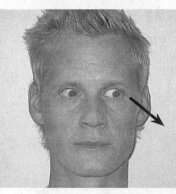

TALKING TO YOURSELF, NEUTRAL

This model has often been misunderstood. The figures in the EAC model have often been interpreted as showing how we all organize our thoughts. But Bandler and Grinder only intended the model as an example, albeit one that applies to many people. In their own words, from the book *Frogs into Princes*: "You will find people who are organized in odd ways. But even somebody who is organized in a totally different way will be systematic; their eye movements will be systematic *for them*."

Anybody who doesn't follow this system will always have his own model, however, and it is easy to discover with the help of some control questions. There will be more about that later on. Note that I am using the word "model" here. That is because this is, necessarily, a simplification and generalization. If, after asking some control questions, you notice that the person you're talking to doesn't seem to follow the model, don't use it. Remember the words of Erickson: "If . . . it doesn't work, . . . do something else." Despite this, the EAC model seems to be useful most of the time. There really seems to be something to that old chestnut about the eyes being the windows of the soul. Or windows of the mind, at least.

What the common model says, then, is this: people who think in images look up and to the left when they are remembering, and up and to the right when they are constructing new images in their minds. An example of a new, constructed, image-based thought would be if you imagined the *Mona Lisa* as having been painted by a five-year-old. (Please note that this is different from the popular, but grossly overgeneralized notion that people look to the right when they lie.) The glance for auditory thoughts is straight to the sides: to the left for memories (like when you're thinking about what somebody said to you), to the right for new thoughts (like when you imagine what you'd like somebody to say to you). Physical sensations and emotions are located down and to the right.

Unfortunately, there is no separation into memory and construction for these kinds of experiences. When internal reasoners (neutral or digital people) talk to themselves to solve logical problems, they will look down and to the left.

If you ask a friend how her holiday was, and she first glances up and to the left, and then quickly down and to the right, you know she is first thinking back to *how it looked,* and then confirming that memory by remembering *how it felt*—assuming she is following the example model!

If you have encountered the EAC model before, you might very well have heard that it is all bunk. But the truth is actually a little more nuanced. Most disprovals of the model are actually disprovals of the notion that you can see whether people are lying by observing their eye movements. However, this is a claim that the creators of the model never made. Other disprovals concern the fact that the model doesn't apply to everyone. The creators would agree. Their point, again, was only that we are all systematic, and never that we are all organized in the same way. In a study, body-language expert Kevin Hogan concluded that we might not even be particularly organized to begin with. However, Hogan himself expresses concerns about the methodology he used, and notes that his study needs to be repeated before the results can be taken to be conclusive. Also, formal neurological research has revealed a connection between mental states and eye movements, which seems to lend support to the ideas behind the EAC model. Personally, all I can do is judge the model based on my own experiences of using it in practice, which have been more than satisfactory. I trust that this is what will matter the most to you, as well. If it works for you— use it!

THE DA VINCI TEST (EXERCISE)

Test the EAC model and find out if it works. You can do it right now. Fix your eyes on a point and to the left and try to visualize the famous painting the *Mona Lisa*. You've seen it many times, even though you may never have given it any special kind of attention. Try to include as many details as you can. The face, the clothes, colors, background details, and so on. Give yourself twenty to thirty seconds to do this. Done? Good. Erase the picture from your mind. Now, fix your eyes down and to the right, and do the same thing. Try to imagine the *Mona Lisa*.

Even though you just did it, and thus shouldn't have any trouble visualizing it again, it's a lot more difficult this time. Right? If so, it is because the visual part of your brain isn't activating as well. I'll put it simply: we don't keep images down and to the right. We keep images up and to the left.

Control Questions

To make sure the EAC model really applies to somebody, you can ask control questions that cause a person to think about specific sensory impressions, and then look at her eyes as she answers. Here are some examples of control questions and prompts:

Visual Memory
How does the carpet in your living room look?
What color is your car?
Describe how your best friend looks.

Visual Construction
How would you look with long/short hair?

Imagine painting your house with stripes.
How would you write your name upside down?

Auditory Memory

How does your favorite song begin?
Imagine the sound of your alarm clock going off.
Do you remember exactly what she said before she left?

Auditory Construction

Can you imagine Barack Obama on helium?
What kinds of voices do you think Laurel and Hardy had?
How would Bruce Springsteen sound under water?

Kinesthetic Memory

Do you remember how hot it was last summer?
How does a pair of ripe old socks smell?
Imagine eating a lemon.

Talking to Yourself (Internal Dialogue)

Can you ask yourself if you often speak to yourself?
What do you say when you're completely alone and something goes wrong?

Speech and Understanding

How Our Senses Affect Our Language

Another way of finding out which kinds of sensory impressions somebody prefers is to listen to the person speak. Speech is full of predicates, words that describe actions, and metaphors, images and similes we use to describe things. According to writers Joseph

O'Connor and John Seymour, the kind of sensory impression we prefer determines the kinds of words and phrases we use in our speech.

Visual Words

A visual person uses words that make sense in visual contexts. She prefers words like: *look, focus, picture, portray, insight, shiny, visualize, perspective, see, foresee, clarify, illustrate, reveal, illusion, show, vision, light.*

She uses expressions like:

I need to take a closer look at this.
I see your point.
I want to see you.
Show me what you mean.
In ten years, you'll look back at this and laugh.
The future looks bright.
She's a colorful person.
Without a shadow of a doubt.
This has tinted your opinions.
Like a flash of lightning from a clear blue sky.

Auditory Words

An auditory person will use different words that ring true to her: *say, emphasis, rhythm, loud, tone, monotonous, deaf, ring, ask, tell, discuss, comment, audible, listen, mute, screaming, dissonant, voice, harmonious.*

She says things like:

Listen to what I have to say.
He voices his opinions.
What a loud color!

We're on the same wavelength.
Living in harmony with nature.
It rings a bell.
Word for word.
I've never heard anything like it.
I think I speak for all of us.
So to speak.

Kinesthetic Words

A kinesthetic person (most often a touch- or emotions-oriented person, but in this context also one whose primary sense is taste or smell) feels the most comfortable using terms like: *touch, handle, press, tight, warm, cold, contact, tension, stress, solid, sore, hold, grasp, tangible, heavy, light, even, hard, sour, juicy.*

She will emphasize expressions such as:

Get a taste of this.
That stinks.
Are we going to rush into something new?
It finally sunk in.
Between a rock and a hard place.
I could feel it all over my body.
We've only scratched the surface.
I can't quite pin it down.
He's a fragile personality.
A good foundation to work from.
She's sweet.

Neutral Words

Finally, a neutral person, who prefers internal dialogue with words that are not related to the senses, like: *decide, determine, think, remember, know, note, understand, estimate, alert, process, motivate, learn, change, aware, able, statistically, logically.*

I cannot give you a list of metaphors since neutral people stay away from those expressions as much as possible. You could sum it up by saying they speak more or less like an academic paper.

The irony is that in their efforts to avoid being misunderstood, neutral people leave themselves open to interpretation. Since the people listening often do so from the point of view of a different sensory impression, they are free to interpret the message, often altering the original message somewhat. By avoiding using words associated with sensory impressions, the "neutrals" also tend to make their own speech much harder to understand, since it becomes more abstract without the sensory words. After all, we use sensory words to make things easier to understand, by comparing things to something we have a direct relationship to, like seeing, feeling, or hearing something.

As you may have started to suspect, our primary sense affects not only our linguistic practices but also what will receive our attention and seem significant to us. If a visual person, an auditory person, and a kinesthetic person went to a concert together and were asked what it was like, their conversation could sound something like the following. Can you guess who's who?

- "They had rearranged all of the songs, very exciting. Great PA, but I wonder why they had to play so loud?"
- "I couldn't see much, but it was a great stage show. The finale was incredibly sparkly."
- "I thought it was very crowded and warm, but it was still an experience that had a great impact on me."
- Asked why he wasn't allowed to go with them, their friend mumbled, "I've been asking myself the same thing."

Our Senses Determine Who We Are

Even such basic things about ourselves as our chosen occupations are affected by which primary sense we have. Architects need to be good at visualizing complex three-dimensional models. To be able to do this, they need a well-developed visual sense. Just about every music producer is an auditory person. A good athlete needs to be kinesthetic to have the right kind of awareness of her body. Neutral or internal people make good lawyers. Studies made concerning people's chosen professions have shown that this is not just an interesting theory, but actually corresponds to fact.

Knowledge of the primary sense of the person you're communicating with can be used to adapt what you say to her. Completely different things and experiences can be significant in the life of a visual person as opposed to a kinesthetic or auditory person. Find out which kind of sensory impressions she prefers, and use the words she would use. A visual person should be asked if she's *seen* the advantages; an auditory person needs to *hear* about all the benefits; and a kinesthetic person needs to know that it *feels* right. Use metaphors and descriptions the same way, and make sure you are talking about the kinds of things you know are important to her. In other words, the things she herself focuses on, listens for, and puts weight on. With a visual person, you want to speak in images, painting pictures of bright futures, how to focus on your vision and not lose perspective. There's no use telling a visual person she needs to build a solid foundation to avoid future pitfalls. Those are kinesthetic words, and she won't understand what you mean. I'm sure you've been in a situation where you're arguing with somebody who really seems to mean the same thing you do, but you still can't agree. Often, it goes like this:

HIM: "But can't you see what I mean?"

YOU: "Yes, I hear what you're saying, but I don't understand your argument."

You're simply speaking different languages. But now you can adapt your speech to the way the other person understands, thinks about, and communicates to the world:

HIM: "But can't you see what I mean?"

YOU: "Okay, I'll give this a really good look this time."

Lots of Them

Rapport with Several People at Once

If you're communicating with several people at once, at a meeting for instance, you should make sure you use in your communication all the different sensory impressions. Let's say you're giving a presentation. Apart from telling the audience about your topic (for the auditory people), make sure you always use a lecture pad or Power-Point presentation (for the visuals) and have hard copies of your document (for the kinesthetics to hold on to). For the neutral people, make sure your arguments are logical and easy to follow. In this way you can maximize everybody's potential for understanding. Also, make sure the expressions you choose switch between the various kinds of sensory words. Look over your most important points and write up a script in advance. If all you do is express yourself as usual, a large number of people in the audience, the ones who don't have the same primary sense as you do, will have a harder time understanding what you're trying to communicate. When you have something important to say, make sure you say it four times, once for each group of sensory impressions: "I hope you can *see* how important it is to *focus* on this, for you to *hear* what I *say* to you, and that you *can feel the weight* of my arguments—and for that to be the basis of a *rational choice*."

> Try it out in real life! Before reading any further, put this book down, go out of your house (or office) and talk to people. Take care to notice what each person's dominant sense is and adjust your communications accordingly. The rest of the book will be a lot more fun for you if you do.

Dominant Senses

How to Find Somebody's Dominant Sense

Sometimes, it can be hard to identify somebody's primary sense through the EAC model or by listening for words. People who do not have a strong primary sense will use the various types of words to more or less the same degree. And there are always some people that are simply difficult to decode.

Ask Open Questions

You can simply come out and ask the person, "How would you like me to present this to you?" People are often sufficiently aware of their preferences to be able to give you a useful answer to that question. Some will ask you to tell them what you want to say. Others will ask you to write it down and give them some diagrams or pictures to look at. Still others will tell you that the most important thing is for them to get a good feeling of the situation so they will know they can trust you.

You can also use the old car-salesman trick of asking control questions and listening to the answers. Start by asking, "Does this look good to you?" If you don't get a meaningful response, switch to "What aspects of this have you discussed before?" or "I'd like to know how you feel about this." Pay attention to which kinds of questions works best, and then continue to use those kinds of words and expressions.

Note Physical Attributes

Harling and Nyrup, whom we discussed earlier, note that certain physical attributes are connected to preferred sensory impressions. I want to be very clear about the fact that what you are about to read includes some very broad generalizations. These are the most apparent in people with extremely dominant primary senses, but they still work quite well as part of a template for a rough first impression of somebody, before you've had the time to observe the person closer.

Strongly *visual* people care a lot about how things—themselves especially—look. They are very observant of colors, shapes, and lighting. A strongly visual person is fast-paced. Since images come quicker to her than words do, a visual person needs to speak quickly to keep up, and she will often do so in a clear, fairly strong voice. Her high tempo of speech will in turn cause her to breathe faster, at the top of her chest, since she never has time to rest properly. Her body language will follow her words and be fast and jerky. Since visual memory is activated by looking up a little, you'll often find visual people's eyes in that position, although they will often take care to maintain eye contact with the person they're speaking to.

Visual children trying to figure out the answer to a question in school would often be told, "The answer isn't written on the ceiling!" by their teachers. This would, of course, lead to them not being able to answer the question, as they had to keep looking straight ahead.

An extremely *tonal* or *auditory* person thinks at the same tempo at which he speaks. This means he has a slower tempo than a visual person. He moves with focus but in a relaxed way, and gestures will often be made around the midsection. Since he uses auditory memories in his thinking, he will also easily be distracted by noises. If you begin talking to a tonal person who is trying to figure something out, he will often lose track of his thoughts. Like myself, for instance. Anybody who talks to me while I am measuring scoops of coffee has ruined the next pot for sure. An auditory person will often slant his head when he thinks, as if he is listening for something. He'll breathe with his diaphragm and speak melodically, in a rhythmic, varied voice.

A strongly *kinesthetic* person is very aware of how things feel, both inside and outside. The kinds of things a kinesthetic person will pay attention to are the sun glaring in her eyes, her seat being hard to sit on, and her sweater feeling cozy. Or that it's a little warm, but that, on the whole, she feels good. A strongly kinesthetic person has a slow tempo. Before she says anything, she has to be sure it feels right. She speaks slowly, softly, and deeply, or in a thin, high voice. Her body language will often be minimal, and whatever of it she displays will be slow and revolve around the stomach area. A kinesthetic person breathes with her stomach, which is what everybody is really designed to do. Eye contact isn't as important for taking in other people, but touch is more important. The archetype for a kinesthetic person would be Santa Claus, an overweight man with a beard in a thick sweater. Or the Betty Crocker–esque mom stereotype.

No corresponding characteristics have been found for the *neutral* or *internally reasoning* people. Many neutral people look like kinesthetics, but far from all do. There is a theory that attempts to explain this connection. The idea is that since our kinesthetic senses, i.e., the bodily and emotional ones, are some of the first senses we develop, and abstract thinking (the neutral sense) shows up a lot later, some neutrals may have been kinesthetics to start with. An emotional trauma during their first years of life may have caused them to block their emotions behind a wall of abstract and strictly logical reasoning. As far as I can tell, the jury is still out on this theory.

Observe Tempo

What the previous section means, in summary, is that by simply paying attention to somebody's tempo in their speech and body language, you can get an indication of what the person's primary sense is likely to be, even before you've had a chance to follow his or her gaze or listen for specific words. The opposite is true, too. If you know which sense is the primary sense, you will have a good idea of the tempo the person will exhibit in breathing, speech, and motion. A visual person has a fast tempo, a kinesthetic person is slow, and an auditory person is somewhere in between. Knowing all that also means you know what to do. After a little practice you will also be able to follow the other person's eye movements as she thinks. If a visual has her eyes pointed up and to the right as she describes something to you, you can mirror her thought process and move your own eyes the same way. This will give you the feeling that you're seeing the same image she is. In the same way, you can listen for the same sounds or try to feel the same thing that the person you're talking to is hearing or feeling. This isn't something we pay conscious attention to, but it registers unconsciously and strengthens the sense of belonging and rapport.

If you understand what kind of sensory impressions the other person prefers, you'll understand what he's trying to say to you. By adapting your choice of words to the way the other person thinks and perceives the world, you can express yourself without any danger of being misunderstood. But more important, you will express yourself like he does and talk about the kinds of things he finds meaningful. This shows him you think the same way, and at the same time it provides you with a fantastic and intimate insight into how his mental processes function.

Earlier, I told you to follow external behavior like body language, tone of voice, tempo, and energy levels to establish rapport. With your new understanding of dominant senses and the EAC model, you can even adapt to the way the other person thinks. You might think that will make you as good a mind reader as you can get. But it doesn't stop there. There is something else that affects our mental processes: our emotions. The way we feel at the moment has an impact on what goes through our heads and also determines how we interpret our experiences, like our encounters with other people. Fortunately, just as with body language and primary senses, we can also observe what other people are feeling, even when they try their hardest to hide it. In the next chapter, I'll teach you how to do that, what different emotional expressions signify, and what to do when you've identified one.

A Curious Thing

Before we end this chapter, I have one more thing to add regarding the use of different words for different sensory systems. I decided to include this section later in the book because I hope that by now you might have had the time to go out and use the model.

If not, please do.

If you already have, I'm sure you will have experienced good results.

And if that is the case, you might be interested to learn that I just might have told you a big fat lie.

Since the theory about dominant senses was first suggested, a fair amount of research has been done in the field. And the general consensus seems to be that although we do use our five senses when we communicate, we do not necessarily have a dominant sense that is stable over time and can be identified by our choice of words. Which one of our senses will be dominant depends on the specific situation we are asked to use it in. And even then, we frequently switch between our temporarily dominant sense and the other ones. There is also little to no evidence to support the notion that we learn or understand things any better when someone matches their communication to our dominant sense.

Whoops.

But if that is true, how can it be that so many people, from therapists to teachers to business leaders—possibly even yourself, assuming you tried it—claim to have achieved highly positive results using the model of dominant senses? Are they all the victims of self-delusion? Possibly. Or perhaps they are right and the current research findings will turn out to be false. Stranger things have happened. But let me offer another possible explanation: perhaps, by searching for patterns such as these, you become much more focused and receptive to subtle nuances in other peoples' communication *in general,* and perhaps this also gives you a more acute sense of what they are trying to tell you on a deeper level, regardless of how they're actually doing it. Maybe, by actively trying to communicate better with someone, you are doing precisely that. So whatever the truth may be, there's really no reason to stop paying close attention to what other people are saying to you—and how they are saying it. As you have, no doubt, already found out for yourself.

5

Emotions

HOW WE ALWAYS REVEAL OUR EMOTIONS

*In which emotions are deromanticized, we are attacked by
a tiger, and we attentively study a myriad of muscle movements.*

Our emotions are an important part of who we are. We often allow our emotions to control our decisions and actions. That is, we don't always do things because we ought to; sometimes we are led by our emotions (or at least this is how we rationalize our behavior after the fact). Sometimes, we're not even aware of the emotions we're having. However, and fortunately for us mind readers, human beings always reveal their emotions, even when they are aware of them or want to hide them. Understanding how other people filter or interpret their experiences and impressions makes up a great part of mind reading. Dominant senses are one of the keys you need to unlock those secrets. To be able to see what emotional state another person is in is another big part of that puzzle.

Once More, With Feeling!

What Exactly Is an Emotion?

Everyone knows what an emotion is, until asked to give a definition. —BEVERLEY FEHR AND JAMES RUSSELL

Before we study the actual facial expressions involved, I think we would do well to get clear on the concept of "emotions" first. What exactly is an emotion? Many theories have been suggested about our emotions and their sources. What has been established is that all people have the same basic emotions, and that they are triggered by the same things.

Emotions as a Survival Mechanism

The most common cause of an emotion is a feeling or belief that we are being threatened, either in terms of our personal safety or in terms of our general well-being. A popular theory, therefore, posits that the origins of emotions are as biological survival mechanisms, that they are shortcuts that override rational deliberations in situations where there simply isn't enough time to figure things out properly. In certain situations, we need to be able to react immediately, automatically, just to survive. If you were a Stone Age human and had to go through an intentional analysis of all of the implications of a large tiger lunging right at you, and you had to consider your different options for getting out of the situation, you'd end up a tiger's snack. The idea is that we're always, unconsciously, scanning the environment for certain events and signs. If a specific sign is observed, that triggers an emotion that is connected to that particular signal. A message is passed on to the autonomic nervous system to activate certain processes, while the same message is transmitted to our conscious mind to tell us what is about to happen. In case you're interested, here's how it happens in more detail:

There are two paths emotional information can take through the brain. They both start off at the same point: our receptors have received a signal and sent it to a part of the brain called the thalamus. From there, the signal is passed on to the amygdala, which is a small, almond-shaped part of the brain and is thought to be involved in emotional reactions. The amygdala is connected to the parts of the brain that control pulse, blood pressure, and other reactions in the autonomic nervous system. However, there are different routes to take to get to the amygdala. One of them is an expressway straight to the amygdala, which causes an immediate reaction that triggers the autonomic nervous system but without giving us any real idea of what it's really reacting to. The other way travels through more densely populated areas and is a little slower. First, it moves to the part of the brain that has to do with attention and thinking (the cerebral cortex) before it moves on to the amygdala. This takes longer but gives us more of an idea of what the signal means.

In purely practical terms, this means that if something big comes roaring toward us at great speed, that's a stimulus that will trigger the emotion *fear*. Fear means, among other things, that the pulse is elevated and that blood is pumped into the large muscles in our legs to prepare us to run away if we need to. Since the body reacts before the mind does, you will have made the evasive maneuver and driven your car off the road before you have time to think, "Shit! That truck is driving on the wrong side of the road!" Or perhaps you realize you were just jumping at a shadow, and now you're up to your waist in mud for no good reason.

Your body will take longer to return to its normal state than it does for your thoughts to do so. This means that despite the danger being averted, your heart will keep racing and you'll have a dry mouth for a while, whether it's called for or not.

In other words, emotions started as part of an automated system to get us out of threatening situations. They cause necessary changes to different parts of our brains and affect our autonomic nervous system, which in turn regulate functions like breathing, sweating, and heart rates. But emotions also alter our facial expressions, our voices, and our body language.

 Emotions started out as automatic mechanisms for starting up the autonomic nervous system without our first needing to think about what is going on. In this way, they aided in our survival and subsequent evolution into a nearsighted, thin-skinned, and slow biped.

We're not emotional all the time. Emotions come and go, and sometimes they replace one another. Some people are more emotional than others, but even they have spells when they are not filled with any particular emotions. There is a difference between an emotion and a mood. An emotion is shorter, and more intense, while a mood can last a lifetime and serves as a "background" to your emotions.

Before psychology matured into a scientific field of its own, emotions were considered psychologically insignificant. Darwin concluded that many of our emotional expressions no longer fill any function, as they are still used in the same way as they were when we swung from tree to tree. They're simply remains from an era when humans were more-primitive beings. Most writers on the subject agreed that emotions would become less important as time goes by and would eventually disappear as humans develop. Sounds pretty boring, huh? Fortunately, contemporary scientists disagree. Today, we understand that our emotions actually have center stage in all human life. For it is our emotions that tie together all the things that are important to us about other people, events, and the world.

When we have an emotion, we say we "feel" something. What we're actually "feeling" are these triggered, physical reactions occurring within us. Some of the changes are straining and unpleasant, especially those that require great bodily exertion. Other changes are a lot more pleasant. They are what we would consider positive emotions. But the experience we are referring to when we say we "feel" joy or anger is actually our experience of the automated biological reactions occurring within us. It may sound a bit dry or unromantic, and I'm sorry if I've demystified another vague term. First "mind reading" and now "emotions"! But if you think about it, their significance isn't reduced at all. Emotions (and mind reading, too) are still as fantastic and amazing as before. Because even if you now know the reason why your body tingles every time you look at your special friend, that it's just a side effect of an automated biological reaction, that still doesn't change the fact that you actually *feel* that warm, wonderful tingle in every part of your body!

Other Emotional Triggers

Of course, we're not struggling for our lives every time we have an emotion. Our emotions have developed over time, grown more numerous, and become more sophisticated. Not all emotions are universal; some are only shared with other people from the same culture. Emotions can also be triggered in other ways than the purely automatic ones. Renowned psychologist Paul Ekman has studied the effects various mental states have on us and how they are reflected in our bodies and faces. He has identified nine different ways of triggering an emotion:

- **AAAH! Tiger Ahead!** The most common way for an emotion to be triggered is once the correct sign is detected in our surroundings. The problem is that we don't have time to reflect on whether or not the emotion is an appropriate reaction. We could be mistaken, after all. Maybe the tiger was just a rock. And we just threw our best spear at it.

- **I Wonder Why She Did That?** We can trigger emotions by thinking about whatever is happening. When we comprehend it, it clicks with our emotional database, and the automated process kicks in. The mistakes will be fewer, but it takes longer. ("Aha—it was a tiger after all! Just as I thought. Hmmm, now it's eating my leg.")

- **Do You Remember Falling in Love for the First Time?** We can make ourselves emotional by remembering situations where we felt strong emotions. We can either begin feeling the way we did then or feel new emotions as a reaction to what we felt then. We might be disappointed now at how angry we were earlier. This is called an *anchor,* and we will get back to this.

- **Wouldn't It Be Nice If . . .** Our imagination allows us to create imaginary scenes or thoughts, which can awaken emotions in us. It's easy enough to imagine what it would be like if you, say, were ridiculously in love. Try it for yourself. You know, when it feels just *so* amazing. Remember that feeling? Can you feel it now? I thought so.

- **Oh, I Don't Want to Talk About It. It'll Only Get Me All Upset Again.** Sometimes it's enough for us to just sit and talk about how angry we were and we can get angry all over again. Talking about emotional experiences you had in the past can bring the emotions back, even when you don't want them back.

- **HA HA HA HA!!!** It's always more fun to watch a comedy with somebody who laughs than with somebody who's depressed. We can get emotions through empathy, which is when we see somebody experience an emotion and it spreads to us and we feel the same way. That person's emotion can awaken other emotions in us, as well; for instance, we could respond with fear to somebody else's anger.

- **No! Naughty! No Touching the Stove!** The things parents and other authority figures tell us to be afraid of or to like, early on in our lives, will receive the same responses from us when we've grown up. Children also take over feelings by imitation, by seeing how adults react in different situations.

- **Hey, Get in Line Like the Rest of Us!** People who transgress our social norms provoke strong emotions. The norms will vary in different cultures, of course, and failing to follow one of them can elicit anything from disgust to joy, depending on what the norm is and who is overstepping it.

- **Chin Up!** Since emotions have clear physical expressions, we can also trigger an internal, mental experience by consciously using our muscles (especially in our faces) in the way we would *if we did* have the particular emotion, and thus trigger the emotion within us in this way. You tried this for yourself at the beginning of this book when you tried getting angry, remember? The energy exercise you did earlier also works this way, even though that involved your whole body.

Don't Make Faces at Me!

Our Unconscious Facial Expressions

In the movie *The Prestige,* Rebecca Hall's character is married to a magician, played by Christian Bale. Sometimes he tells the truth when he says he loves her, and sometimes he's lying. One of the major themes of the movie is how she can always tell which it is by looking at his eyes.

When we're not sure what somebody really means, we look the person in the eyes. We learn to do that before we learn to walk, although it's really more than the eyes we're looking at, whatever we may believe. The fact is, we examine the whole face closely. There are more than forty muscles in the face, many of which we can't control consciously, and we use them to express very detailed information about ourselves. This means we always reveal things about ourselves, even when we're trying not to. It's actually quite ironic that we're not better at reading these things than we actually are.

Lots of Little Emotions

We have a pretty good ability to tell when somebody is happy or really angry. But often we miss things completely and don't realize somebody is upset until she is bawling right in front of us. We also often get facial expressions mixed up and might believe somebody is afraid when he's really just surprised, or that somebody is angry when he's really just concentrating on a problem. It doesn't help that a change in somebody's face can mean one thing if it is a conscious illustration of what is being said, and something else entirely if it is unconscious. If I am telling you something and you raise your eyebrows, it could mean that you want to show me that you are doubtful or questioning something I am saying. But it could also be an expression of genuine surprise. A crooked smile could be used to show that I understood you were making a joke, but it could also be an unconscious expression of contempt. Things get really messy when we express several things at once with our faces.

Often, we display two emotions at once. If we're surprised and then get happy when we realize what the surprise is all about, we will express surprise followed by joy. In between the two, there is a stage at which we exhibit both the previous and the newer emotions. We will look surprised and happy at the same time. Or, we may experience a genuine mixed emotion, like the great blend of fear and joy we get from a good roller-coaster ride. We also often try to hide our true feelings, and display something else instead, like when we're sad but try to look happy. In cases like this, the hidden emotion will almost always seep through, which means we are unconsciously displaying both the emotion we're trying to conceal and the one we're pretending to have instead. Sometimes, we will use our facial expressions as comments, not simply to what we're saying, but even to our other facial expressions! An example of this would be when we look sad, but squeeze a smile out to show we'll be OK. Maybe it's not so strange that we get things mixed up after all.

Emotions Make Us Human

Looking people in the eyes is a good idea, as I said. After all, our many different facial expressions reveal our humanity. It is a well-known piece of Hollywood lore by now that George Lucas covered the eyes and faces of the storm troopers in *Star Wars* with plastic helmets in order to make them seem less human. In the present day, we encounter real-life versions of Lucas's storm troopers, thanks to the use of the popular nerve toxin Botox. This is something more and more people who are past their middle age are happily injecting into themselves—more specifically, into their faces. Botox causes local paralysis (it is a nerve toxin, after all), which smooths out wrinkles. Unfortunately, it also means you can no longer use some of your facial muscles, as they are paralyzed. This means you're not only getting the skin of a Barbie doll, you're getting its range of facial expressions, too.

I once spoke to a store manager in New York who explained that Botox was starting to turn into a real problem for him, since he spends a lot of time in negotiations. He can't read his clients' reactions to the different propositions he presents to them, since they have no capacity for nuanced facial expressions. He told me he found talking to many of them disquieting. They feel artificial, inhuman, as their faces stay the same whether they are angry or happy.

Here's a tip: if you want to be understood, try not to inject nerve toxins in your face.

By paying attention to the changes in somebody's face, we can receive information not only about her present emotions but also about the emotions she is *about to begin* feeling. The fact is, since muscles react quicker than the mind does (I'll explain this in more detail in a while), you can see which emotion is starting to show in somebody, even before she is aware of it herself. That is, before she starts "feeling" it. This is useful if this is an emotion that isn't very useful in the situation you're in, an emotion like anger or fear, for instance. If you see early signs of an emotion like that, you still have an opportunity to help the person avoid that state. Once the emotion has had time to kick in, it will be a lot more difficult, often even impossible, to do anything about it.

Othello's Mistake

The big problem about emotions is that once we have one, it's very hard to think in ways that don't confirm the emotion. We are "slaves to passion," which is quite a good description really. Our memories and our impressions of the world suddenly become very selective. When you are filled with an emotion, it will stop you from remembering things you actually know but that would contradict the emotion. What you do manage to remember is often distorted. In the same way, you will perceive the world as filtered by that emotion. If it is a negative emotion, you won't see potential positive possibilities and openings. On the other hand, you get very good at perceiving anything that confirms your feelings. You will also suddenly remember things you left behind years ago but that also strengthen the emotion: "And by the way, do you remember that thing you did eight years ago?!" Sound familiar? When we have a strong emotion, we're simply not looking to challenge it. On the contrary, we want to strengthen and maintain it. Sometimes this helps us, but it will often cause problems. Our friend Paul Ekman has referred to this as *Othello's mistake,* named for the jealous main character in *Othello* by William Shakespeare (there he is again!).

In the play, Othello is convinced that his beloved Desdemona has betrayed him and made out with another guy called Cassio, which makes Othello furious. (Cassio is Othello's best friend, and the whole thing is actually a lie from the evil Iago—Othello's other best friend. Seems our Othello isn't too bright when it comes to picking friends.) Othello is beside himself with jealous rage and threatens to kill Desdemona. Des tells Othello to go ask Cassio, and he'll find out his suspicions are wrong, but that's no help, because Othello tells her he's already killed Cassio. When Desdemona realizes there is no longer any way for her to prove her innocence, she literally fears for her life. Since Othello is stuck in his emotional state, with an extremely selective perception of the world, he interprets her reaction incorrectly. He fails to realize that even an innocent person would react with stress and fear in this kind of situation. And, as the Bard put it, "men in rage strike those that wish them best." Othello considers her emotional reactions evidence that she actually did have something to hide, so he smothers her with a pillow.

It's easy to think of Othello as a brute or a romantic fool, but the truth is that he got caught in the same trap we all do when we're in a strong emotional state. It is extremely difficult to see yourself and your actions objectively when you are filled up with emotion. It takes a lot of training. For this reason, it is valuable for you to learn to recognize it when people are heading into a negative emotional state, so you can slow it down before it kicks in properly.

Do you remember I told you how you could lead somebody with your body language to get the person into a better mood? When you alter a person's emotional state, you are also helping him or her replace that negative selective perception with a more positive one. The negative point of view can be replaced by a more positive outlook, which is a much more useful way to look at yourself and your situation.

 Strong emotions can distort your perceptions of the world. Negative emotions block off potentially positive experiences, and promote forgotten, negative thoughts. Don't do anything you might regret later on if you're stuck in a strong emotion. Try to wait until the emotion has passed before you act, even if it's difficult to do so.

Unconscious Information

You can tell when somebody is getting upset or angry, afraid or hostile, even before she actually is, by being observant of her facial expressions. This way, you will know what somebody is about to feel even before she feels it. This is top-level mind reading, so you should be careful about how you handle the information you get. These are things the person you're talking to hasn't consciously decided to share with you, and it is information of a personal nature. The mere fact that you have insight into somebody's emotional life doesn't automatically constitute an invitation into her most intimate spaces. Simply blurting out what you've noticed about the person can be taken as a great intrusion of privacy, and it can completely destroy any rapport you have going. For this reason, it's often best to let what you see determine the choices you make in your communication, rather than confronting it head on.

The Seven Samurai

Seven Universal Emotional Expressions

When Ekman traveled around the world to study how we express emotions, he found seven basic emotions that we all display in the same way, whether we live in Papua New Guinea or in Springfield, Idaho. The seven basic emotions are:

Surprise
Sadness
Anger
Fear
Disgust
Contempt
Joy

Of course, there are more emotions than this group of seven; for instance, "joy" is better understood as a cluster concept consisting of several positive emotions, rather than as a single specific one. But the emotions that aren't on the list can be expressed in different ways, or triggered by different things, depending on the culture and place we live in. For our present purposes, however, these seven emotions will suffice.

Ekman performed a systematic analysis of how each emotion affects the facial muscles, that is, how we look when we're experiencing different emotions. I have used Ekman's model as the starting point for the images that will follow, and for clarity's sake I have used full, strong facial expressions. You won't see this kind of emotional expression much in real life. It is more common for somebody to display only part of an expression, and in a much more subtle way than in the following images. But once you know what to look for, even subtly expressed emotions will be easily detected.

Subtle changes in the face can reveal which emotion a person is heading into, even before he knows it himself, or even when he's never aware of it himself at all. But it could also be that he is very well aware of what he is feeling, and is doing everything he can to hide it by displaying a different emotion or none at all. The subtle, unconscious expressions are your clues to what he is really feeling. I will also describe what goes on in your face when you're trying not to reveal your true emotions.

Three Kinds of Subtle Expressions

There are three main classes of subtle emotional facial expressions: *slight expressions, partial expressions,* and *microexpressions*.

A *slight* expression uses the whole face, but without much intensity. All of the different parts of the face are involved, but the change isn't very obvious. A slight expression can signal a weak emotion, which can in turn be either weak in general or simply weak at the moment. It might be a strong emotion, which has recently begun and isn't fully developed yet, or simply a previously strong emotion that is ebbing out. A slight expression can also be the result of a failed attempt to consciously conceal a strong emotion—like when the runner-up on *American Idol* hugs the winner, trying really hard not to look disappointed.

A *partial* expression will only use one or two of the parts of the face required for a complete facial expression. These partial expressions can be strong or slight but will most commonly be slight. A partial expression also signals one of two things: either it is a genuinely weak emotion, because it is not felt strongly or about to go away, or it can be a failed attempt to hide a strong emotion.

Microexpressions are lightning fast but complete facial expressions that reveal what the person is actually feeling. They can be as brief as a twenty-fifth of a second, and are very difficult to observe consciously. Often they are the results of an interruption. We start exhibiting or feeling fear, notice it, and then try to hide our expressions quickly under a different emotion. But for a brief moment, a complete expression of fear was visible in the whole face. Microexpressions often happen in the middle of other things, like speech, leaning forward, and so on. They are immediately followed by attempts to cover up. Most people don't notice microexpressions, at least not consciously, but anybody with normal eyesight can see them. All it takes is a little training. Microexpressions always signal a repressed emotion, but the expressions don't reveal themselves if the repression is conscious or unconscious, or if the repressed emotion conflicts with the consciously expressed one or not.

The Expression Doesn't Reveal the Cause

Finally, remember, when you spot an emotion, you still have no idea what caused it. Othello forgot about this and interpreted what he saw from his own emotional perspective. If you can tell from somebody's face that she is angry, it doesn't necessarily mean she's angry *at you*. She could be angry at herself or simply remembering a previous occasion when she was angry, which has triggered the same emotion now. Remember the nine emotional triggers discussed earlier in this chapter. So, if you're going to let the emotional expressions you see in others affect your own behavior, you should first make sure you also know the cause of their emotions. The best thing to do is usually to keep quiet about what you've seen and keep an eye out for the opportunities this knowledge will offer you. I will go into more detail on how Ekman suggests you approach each specific emotion, but most of these methods involve giving the other person a subtle opening to express how she feels, rather than a direct confrontation, and the emotion you have noticed is rarely mentioned at all. "I get the impression you might be having some feelings we haven't spoken about yet, is that right?" Sometimes, however, you shouldn't comment at all.

 There are three different categories of subtle facial expressions, which can all indicate a conscious attempt to hide a strong emotion. The first two can also indicate an openly displayed but weak emotion, or that an emotion (which may come to grow strong) has only just been triggered.

1. Slight expressions: The whole expression is displayed, but with low intensity.

2. Partial expressions: Only part of the expression is displayed (the eyebrows, for example).

3. Microexpressions: The whole expression is displayed with intensity, but only for an extremely brief moment.

Neutral

The picture in this section is of me several years ago, on an ordinary morning in November. That's what I look like when my face is completely relaxed. All faces look different, and some have properties that can make you think they are expressing an emotion even when they're not. As you can tell, I have pretty thin lips and a relatively small mouth. The corners of my mouth also have a slight downward curve. This means people who don't know me can often get the idea that I am angry about something when I am simply relaxed, because thin lips is one of the attributes that reveal anger. For this reason, unless it is completely obvious, you should never believe that someone you've just met is in a certain emotional state. It could just be how he or she looks. So, before you can read my emotions, you need to know what I look like when I am relaxed, or you won't have anything to compare my expressions with.

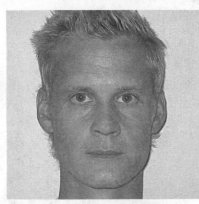

Neutral:

"Oh, look. Another season of The Kardashians.*"*

Each of the following seven emotions will be presented with a picture of a *complete* facial expression in which the emotion is expressed as purely as possible. The expression will, for clarity's sake, be strong, even though these expressions are seldom this strong in everyday life. The complete expression is then broken down into its various components.

Surprise

Surprise is the emotion we feel for the shortest time, so let's begin there. When are we surprised? When something unexpected happens. When what we think is about to happen suddenly turns out to be something else. We mustn't have a clue about what is about to happen, because then we wouldn't be surprised. Surprise only lasts for a few seconds, until we understand what just happened. Then, it turns into another emotion, which is a reaction to the thing that surprised us. At this point, we might say, "What a nice surprise!" But in actual fact, the surprise in itself has no value one way or the other. The joy we feel is what comes after we understand what happened, like an unexpected visitor coming to our house.

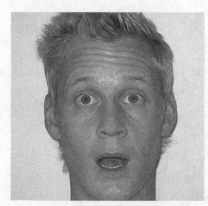

Surprise: complete expression

"OMG!!!"

Since surprise occurs when we're not prepared for it, we basically can never hide it, even if we wanted to. Getting surprised is usually not a problem, unless the object of our surprise was known to us from before, of course.

Surprise doesn't occur just when we're startled and flinch, as we do when we hear loud, unexpected noises, for example. That is simply a physical reflex, which actually looks like the opposite of surprise. We scrunch up our faces and curl up to protect ourselves. When we're surprised, our faces open up as much as they can. Surprise affects three areas in the face in a distinctive way.

Surprise: eyebrows and forehead

The eyebrows are arched up high. More of the skin under the eyebrows will show, and horizontal wrinkles will appear on the forehead of anybody who isn't rather young. People who already have those wrinkles when relaxed will have deeper, more distinctive wrinkles. If somebody just displays his or her eyebrows the way I do in the picture, without corresponding action in the mouth and eyes, it no longer signals surprise. And if the eyebrows stay in place for a few moments, that means you're doubting, questioning or feeling astonished at what you're hearing. It could be a serious expression or not, like in situations where you simply can't believe what you've just been told. As you can see in the picture, my whole face seems to express this kind of questioning attitude, even though the only thing that's different is the eyebrows. The picture is actually a clever montage of the neutral expression and the total-surprise picture. The eyebrows and forehead are taken from the surprised face, and the rest is from the neutral face you saw earlier. All images on the following few pages are made in the same way, with the neutral image used as the base, and the specific parts of the face added in. As you can see, lots of facial expressions are changed completely (and express completely different emotions) when just one small part of the face changes.

It also seems as though a person who is asking a question she already knows the answer to, or who is asking a rhetorical question, will tend to accentuate the question by raising her eyebrows. On the other hand, if she doesn't know the answer, the lowered, contracted eyebrows, which indicate concentration (but are often mistaken for anger), will be displayed. Try it yourself—ask the question "How are we going to solve this?" once with your eyebrows lowered and once with your eyebrows raised. Notice how the question's undertone changes from one of collaborative problem solving (lowered eyebrows) to a much more confrontational one (raised eyebrows).

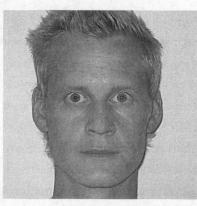

Surprise: eyes

As you can see in the picture, the eyes are open wide. The upper eyelids are raised, but the lower ones are relaxed. The whites of the eyes, above the iris (the colored membrane that surrounds the pupil) will be visible in many people. Sometimes you can also see the white of the eye below the iris, but this depends on how deeply set the eyes are and on whether the skin under the eyes is stretched out when the mouth is open.

The wide-open eyes are most often displayed along with either raised eyebrows or an open mouth or both, but they can also occur in isolation. Then they are part of a very brief expression, one of increasing interest, the kind of thing that makes us say "WOW!"

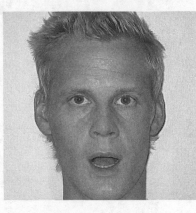

Surprise: mouth

When we first become surprised, our jaw literally drops and our mouth opens. How much depends on the strength of the emotion. Surprise comes in varying degrees of intensity, and how surprised somebody is will often be most clearly expressed by the mouth. Eyes and eyebrows always look more or less the same, but the more open somebody's mouth is, the greater the surprise is. When all you can see is an open mouth, that's what they call being "dumbstruck." It could be an unconscious expression of a legitimate emotion, or a conscious signal that is intended to display the emotion.

When we want to hide our real feelings, we often feign surprise. But real surprise lasts for such a short time, you can't really use it to cover anything up. The clue that gives away feigned surprise is usually that it lasts for too long. Surprise is the quickest emotion and should only be apparent for a few seconds before passing into a different emotion.

Sadness

Sadness or sorrow is one of the longest-lasting emotions. When I use the word "sorrow," I don't mean the sort of extreme expression that sometimes finds an outlet at funerals, for instance. All emotions have an extreme form of expression (the extreme form of fear, for instance, is phobia). What I am referring to are the more-commonplace expressions of emotional states.

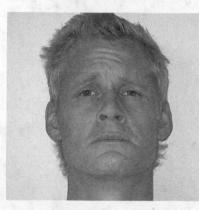

Sadness: complete expression

"You had me at hello."

There are many things that can make us unhappy, but it usually happens when we lose something. It could be that we lose our self-confidence after failing at something at work; we could be rejected by a friend or partner; we could have lost a limb in an accident; someone could have died, of course; or perhaps we've lost some possession that we're particularly fond of. We say that we're feeling low, depressed, sad, disappointed, miserable, helpless, or desperately unhappy. We become passive and withdrawn, which allows us to save our energy and rebuild our strength. But we have a tendency to get sadness and anger mixed up; we become angry with those who have made us unhappy, as a form of defense.

Sadness also has a social function, because a person who displays signs of being sad will often receive help, comfort, and reassurance from others. For some reason, many men absorbed a peculiar tradition when they grew up, that we shouldn't let anybody see that we are sad. A lot of people will therefore do all they can to conceal their feelings when they're sad. But this doesn't mean that they will succeed—they probably won't, because facial expressions occur involuntarily. They appear even when we don't want them to. People who are trying to suppress their emotions almost always show visible leakage.

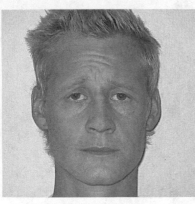

Sadness: eyebrows, forehead, and upper eyelids

In its most extreme form, the only sign of sadness or sorrow could be a lack of muscle tension in the face. But most often there will be a reaction in the brow and forehead. The inner parts of the eyebrows are contracted and raised. Note that the whole eyebrow is not pulled up, just the inner end. This is one of the most difficult muscular movements to make consciously. I call it

"Woody Allen eyebrows," because it seems to be a more or less permanent feature on his face.

The movement of the eyebrows also means that vertical wrinkles between the eyebrows will be created or deepened and that the inner corners of the upper eyelids will be raised and acquire a triangular look. Some people will raise their eyebrows very discreetly. It can be such a slight difference that it is invisible, particularly if the person is trying to hide the expression. But the triangle in the eyelids will still be evident. So if you're not sure, you can always check for that. The opposite holds, too: if you see the triangle in the eyelids of someone who seems to be in a neutral mood otherwise, it's a sure sign that he is starting to feel sad or that he is very sad but trying to hide it as best he can by controlling his facial expression. Apart from this, the eyelids of somebody sad will hang down lower than otherwise. This movement is most often seen alongside the expression in the rest of the face, but it can be displayed alone, like in the picture.

Sadness: lower eyelids

If the sadness is particularly deep, the lower eyelids will also be affected and tense up.

Sadness: mouth

A sad mouth is often confused with the expression used to show contempt. The corners of a sad mouth will point down, and the lower lip might be protruded as we pout. Wrinkles can appear in the skin of the chin. The difference is that when we feel dislike or contempt, our upper lip is raised. Even if the corners of the mouth are turned down, we don't pout with our lower lip when expressing contempt. If only a sad mouth is visible, as in the picture, it's actually impossible to know what the person is really feeling. This is one of the few occasions when a single element of a facial expression isn't enough to tell you what the underlying emotion is.

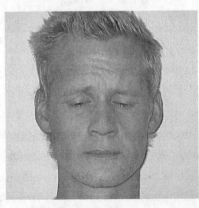

Sadness: looking down

In this picture there is a new characteristic. Lowered eyes are often seen in sad people. Of course, we look down several times a day without necessarily feeling sad, but if we do so while displaying the sad eyebrows, as in the picture, the signs are very clear. Something else that can often happen is for the cheeks to be raised, which makes the eyes narrower than usual.

If someone who isn't sad is pretending to be, she will show it in the lower regions of the face, particularly the mouth, and by looking down. The lack of any signs of sadness in the eyes, eyebrows, and forehead are a good indication that this is a false emotion. (Unless you're dealing with one of those rare people who don't use that part of the face to express sorrow, of course. They do exist, but there aren't many of them.) In order to make sure that it's a genuine expression, you should start by looking for the triangular shape in the upper eyelids.

If someone is feeling sad but trying to hide it, she will generally concentrate on not letting her mouth give her away. The "triangular eye," and usually the eyebrows as well, will still be there for you to recognize.

Anger

The most common reason we get angry is because something or somebody is stopping us from doing what we want to do, when there's somebody in our way. And we get angrier still if the obstacle is meant for us personally. But we can also become frustrated when things don't work the way they should, which is actually just another case of things getting in our way.

We also get angry with ourselves sometimes. Another triggering cause could be violence or threats of violence. That can make us both angry and scared. Of course, we also get angry when people act in ways we disapprove of or let us down. We don't feel

Anger: complete expression, two versions

"I told you to stop hitting your brother!"

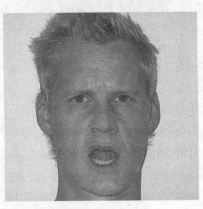

pure anger for particularly long—it tends to get mixed up with some other emotion, like fear or contempt. Anger is the most dangerous emotion, as it can make us try to harm the person we're angry with, physically or emotionally. The urge to want to hurt others arises when we are very young and is something we all have to learn to control as we grow up.

So what is getting angry good for, then? Anger activates us and motivates us to change the thing that has angered us. The problem is to understand just what it was that made us so angry in the first place. Often, we direct our anger toward the wrong things. Taking action when you're angry is almost always a foolish thing to do. When you're angry, everything is interpreted and perceived through that anger. Actually, in these situations, the best thing to do is to shut up and not act at all, until the emotion starts to fade and we become capable of a more nuanced perception of things again.

If we are exposed to any kind of threat, anger can help, too, since it limits fear, and fear can stop you cold. Getting angry will make you deal with the threat instead.

Apart from the other expressions, anger requires a change in all three facial areas. Otherwise, we can't tell if the person is experiencing anger or something else.

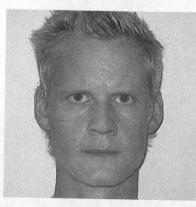

Anger: eyebrows

When we get angry, our eyebrows contract and are lowered. Lines can appear between the eyebrows, but the forehead won't wrinkle. If you see this motion occur on its own, that could mean several different things: the person is angry but trying to hide it; the person is slightly annoyed or starting to get angry; the person is serious or concentrating; the person is confused.

If somebody does this while you're speaking to her, and you haven't just introduced a difficult problem to her, it's a sign you may need to explain yourself more clearly, since she obviously has to concentrate hard to follow what you're saying. Darwin called the muscle responsible for this contraction the "muscle of difficulty." It seems as though we use it anytime we're confronted with something difficult or incomprehensible.

Anger: eyes and eyelids

When we're angry, the eyelids tense up and the eyes become set in a piercing stare. The lower eyelid can be more or less raised, depending on how angry you are. Thanks to the downward pressure from the eyebrow, the upper eyelid looks like it's been lowered, which makes the eyes narrower. If somebody displays these eyes and nothing else, it could mean contained anger, but it could also mean the person is trying to focus or concentrate. Even if the telltale shapes of both eyes and eyebrows are present, the expression could still be one of concentration as well as anger. But when the eyes tense up, it's usually a case of visual concentration more specifically, like when we need to focus our vision on something. To make sure it actually is anger, we also have to be able to see the mouth.

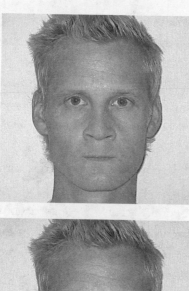

Anger: two different kinds of angry mouths

There are two kinds of angry mouths. The closed one, with the lips pressed together, is used for physical attacks (in a fight) or when you are trying to hold back something you really want to say. Then there is the open mouth, which is used (often loudly) for letting everybody know how angry you are.

If only the mouth is displayed, it's hard to say what it means. A closed mouth can indicate slight anger, or controlled anger, but, just like the eyebrows, it could also indicate concentration or exertion. This time, it's not a case of mental exertion, however. It is physical, like when you lift something heavy.

But the closed, tight mouth is one of the first signs to appear when somebody begins to get angry. It's easy to see the whole jaw section tense up. Often we will display this even before we've noticed that we're getting angry.

It's hard to know if anger is faked, since the expression uses muscles that are easy to control consciously, and everybody knows how to do it. For once, we also tend to remember to use the eyebrows when we fake this emotion. To determine if it's fake, you need to look at timing instead. Is the expression simultaneous with the words or actions, or is it delayed? Anger is actually the best mask to wear to hide another emotion, because we lock up our whole faces, leaving only the eyebrows as clues to our true emotional states. Fortunately, we live in a culture where walking around wearing an angry face all day doesn't help you much, even though some people seem to try. If somebody is angry but tries to hide it, his anger will show through in the tension of his eyelids, his stare, or his contracted eyebrows.

Fear

Fear is the emotion we know the most about, for the simple reason that it is easy to make animals frightened in experiments. Fear is triggered by a danger of harm, physical or emotional. Examples of things that trigger fear are objects moving quickly toward us, or when we lose our footing and fall, both literally and metaphorically. Threats of pain, like knowing you have to go to the dentist, can trigger fear, too. Most, but not all, of us are easily frightened by snakes and reptiles, or of the thought of losing our footing at heights.

In biological terms, fear prepares us for either hiding or running away. Blood flows into the larger muscles in our legs, preparing us to run if we need to. If we don't run, we try to hide. But hiding means doing it the same way animals do, like deer freezing in

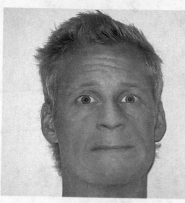

Fear: complete expression

"What? One Direction is back together?"

headlights. That might seem like a strange way to react, but it makes sense, as predators with bad eyesight can't make you out if you don't move. When we say we're going "numb with fear," it's really about hiding.

If we can neither run nor hide, it is very likely our fear will turn into anger instead. So in other words, if the command that orders the nervous system to prepare for flight or hiding doesn't seem useful, we will switch it for one that mobilizes us for action. In order to deal with the situation, we get angry with whatever has threatened us. Our facial expressions when we're afraid signal two things: "There is danger nearby; be careful" and "HEEEELP! GET ME OUT OF HERE!" In this case, it's a good thing we have our facial expressions, because speech often fails us when we get strongly emotional about something. As Winnie the Pooh's friend Piglet put it, "Help, help, a Herrible Hoffalump! Hoff, hoff, a Hellible Horralump! Holl, holl, a Hoffable Hellerump!"

Fear: eyebrows

The eyebrows are raised but stay straight when we display fear. So, as with surprise, the eyebrows are raised but also contracted, which makes the inside corners come closer together than in surprise. They aren't as raised as with surprise, either.

Wrinkles appear in the forehead, too, even though in cases of fear they most often won't go all the way across the forehead. If the eyebrows display without the other facial signals, they signify concern or controlled fear. Now, in this picture, my whole face looks worried, but it is a montage, where everything below the eyebrows is from the original neutral picture.

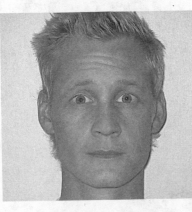

Fear: eyes

The eyes are open and tense. Just as with surprise, the upper eyelids are raised, so we can see the whites of the eyes, but in this case, the lower eyelids are tensed up, instead of being opened, and can cover a portion of the iris. Often, the tense eyes and the raised eyebrows are displayed together (as shown in this case), or with both the eyebrows and the mouth, but they can appear on their own. If that happens, it will be very quick and is an indication of a genuine fear that is either moderate or controlled.

The mouth is open or almost closed. The lips are tense and can be drawn back, as opposed to the more-relaxed mouth we have in surprise. If only the mouth is displayed, it means anxiety or worry. If the closed, fearful mouth is displayed alone, quickly, that can mean you're afraid and trying not to show it, or that you're remembering an occasion when you were afraid, or using it as a conscious illustration in the context of a conversation. Like when you go, "Whoa! That was scary."

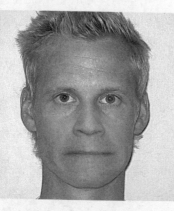

Fear: mouth

When somebody pretends to be afraid, as usual, chances are she will forget to use her eyebrows and forehead and just use the mouth. She'll probably also forget to use her eyes.

If you see just the eyebrows signal fear in somebody's face, perhaps because she is trying to display a different emotion than fear with the rest of her face, that is actually a sufficient and genuine sign of fear. The only time the forehead and eyebrows aren't included in a genuine expression of fear would be when it is a matter of truly paralyzing fear, like in cases of shock. Then, only the eyes and mouth are used.

Disgust

Follow these instructions: swallow once—*now*—to make your mouth dry. Wait for a moment, until you feel you've produced new saliva. It will probably take a little while. Ready? OK? Now imagine spitting this new saliva into a glass.

And then drinking it.

I use this thought experiment, which is inspired by emotions researcher Paul Ekman, when I give lectures. My suggestion is usually met by the facial expression on page 115. Disgust, or revulsion, characteristically involves being repelled by something, like the taste of something you want to spit out right away. Just the thought of eating certain things can make you feel disgust. The same is true of certain smells or the way slimy things feel. Some actions can cause disgust, like mistreating pets or abusing children. The most universal triggers of disgust are actually bodily excretions: feces, bodily fluids, blood, and vomit. The emotion isn't triggered until they exit the body, like in the saliva test mentioned earlier. As long as the saliva was in your mouth, there were no problems. The only difference between the first and second time I asked you to swallow your saliva was that the second time, it had been outside of your body for a short time. And presto! Now you're disgusted!

Disgust doesn't start happening to us until we are four or five years old, but from that point on, it fascinates us completely. That's why novelty stores sell fake vomit, why we like movies like *Dumb and Dumber* and *American Pie,* and why so many people inspect their handkerchiefs after blowing their noses.

As adults, we believe ourselves to mostly feel disgust for other people: people who commit moral wrongs, politicians, bullies, and so on. However, what is considered a moral wrong can vary between different cultures and mind-sets.

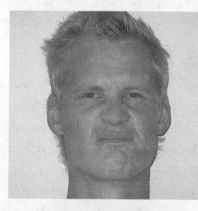

Disgust: complete expression, two versions

"No, really, it's okay. Everybody gets the stomach flu sooner or later."

Disgust is an extremely powerful emotion. Psychologist and re-searcher John M. Gottman spent fourteen years making video-taped interviews with 650 married couples. He and his colleagues at the "Love Lab" discovered that you can find clues as to whether the relationship will last or not in just three minutes of recorded conversation. One of the strongest clues is disgust. If some uncon-scious, subtle sign of disgust is displayed, especially on the woman's part, statistically speaking the couple is not likely to still be mar-ried after four years.

The reason we feel disgust is, naturally, to make us get away from the object of our disgust. One might think that our disgust for blood and bodily waste would have helped us avoid infec-tions, but on the other hand, it has also limited our empathy and social potential. By feeling disgust for other people, we make them less human. This has been (and is still) used to great effect in political and religious propaganda, as we have an easier time being inhuman to people we feel disgust for. Just like in *Star Wars*. Of course, it's a lot easier to kill storm troopers by the dozen if you don't have to see their faces.

In these two pictures, disgust is displayed in the wrinkling of the nose and the raised upper lip. The lower lip can also be raised and protruded, which results in a closed mouth, or low-ered and protruded, which results in an open mouth. In addition to this, wrinkles can appear on the sides of and over the nose. The stronger the disgust is, the more wrinkles will appear. The cheeks will be raised, too, which pushes the lower eyelids up and makes the eyes narrow. This will in turn cause lines and folds under the eyes.

In cases of strong disgust, the eyebrows will often be lowered, but they're actually not too important for this emotional expression. Some people interpret the lowered eyebrows as anger, but they're not contracted at the middle, and the upper eyelids aren't raised, which they would be if this were a case of anger. If we want to express disgust for something, but aren't actually feeling disgust at the moment, we will use parts of the expression. Like wrinkling your nose up and saying, "That really stinks! How often do they clean that hamster cage, anyway?" If we use the whole expression consciously, we will keep it in our faces for longer, to make it clear that we are making a conscious illustration.

Because it is such an obvious expression, disgust is easy to fake, and we often use it for illustrative purposes in conversations. The forehead and eyebrows aren't used much in disgust, which means they won't be missed when somebody fakes it. For this reason, it's also quite easy to conceal disgust, since it is mostly expressed in the lower part of the face.

If you're not sure, look for the wrinkle on the bridge of the nose. It's usually high up enough in the face to avoid any attempts at control. But most often, we don't think of trying to hide this emotion in the first place. I don't think we're always aware of it in the same way we are of other emotions. When you mention "emotions," most people think of sadness, love, anger, and things like that. They will seldom think of disgust. So even when we smile with our mouths, any disgust we're actually feeling will usually have free access to the rest of the face, without us even knowing it.

Contempt

Contempt is closely related to disgust. However, there are a number of significant differences between them, both in how we express them and what they mean. Contempt is only felt for other people and for their actions. Unlike disgust, contempt can't be felt for things. The thought of a techno version of Los del Río's "Macarena" may cause disgust (come to think about it, fear seems a distinct possibility as well), but not contempt. We may, however, feel contempt for those who choose to use a techno version of "Macarena" as their ringtone. We don't necessarily feel the need to get away from people we feel contempt for, but we do feel superior to them. Often, this is a sense of moral superiority.

There is also a classic kind of sociocultural contempt from an inferior position, like the contempt adolescents have for adults, or the uneducated have for academics. This kind of contempt is a way of making yourself feel superior to those who are higher up than you on the social ladder. People who feel insecure about their own positions or status will also often use contempt as a weapon. A lot of people actually maintain power and status by expressing contempt for their inferiors. It's a very effective method, but you tend to get very lonely at the top when nobody likes you.

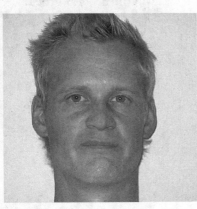

Contempt: complete expression

"What do you mean you don't read books?"

I told you earlier about Gottman's discoveries concerning unconscious signs of disgust in married couples. At that time, it affected a relationship most if the signs came from the woman. Gottman has also measured contempt. When subtle signs of contempt are displayed by the dominant party in the relationship (usually the man), the other party (usually the woman) will feel steamrollered, convinced that the couple's problems can't be solved, that they have serious marital or relationship issues, and she will even get sick more often! This wasn't the case when the subtle expressions were ones of anger or disgust; it was specific to contempt. Therefore, there is every reason to be very aware of this in any kind of relationship.

Some years ago, I was in a relationship that had stagnated. For a few months, I'd grown annoyed with my partner's lifestyle. One day, I realized I was activating particular muscles in my face when I thought of her, making the facial expression for contempt. And this had, naturally, affected my own mental attitudes toward her.

Once I became aware of it, it was easier to avoid that muscular reaction, which caused my perceptions of her and the relationship as a whole to become a lot more positive. It was too late, though, the relationship was already doomed. Of course, there were other reasons why it ended, but my unconscious contempt for who we were in our relationship probably didn't help.

Contempt is displayed in the face with a tightened and raised corner of the mouth. The result is a crooked smile. It can also be a raised upper lip on one side of the mouth, kind of like half a disgust mouth. Imagine Elvis (or Billy Idol). This can be subtle, no more than a twitch in the upper lip, or so obvious that the teeth are showing, depending on how strong the contempt is. The expression is often followed by a rush of air through the nose, a bit like a snort. The eyes tend to turn downward—we literally look down on the person we feel contempt for.

Joy

There are many different positive emotions, just as there are a variety of negative ones. Unfortunately we lack good names for the positives. "Happiness" and "joy" will have to do for now.

Positive emotions include enjoying sensory impressions, like smells or objects of beauty, being amused by something, or simple contentedness. The difference is less obviously displayed in the face and is more reliably identified by voice. Most expressions of joy actually have specific sounds, ranging from squeals of delight to sighs of relief. Other variations of joy are excitement, relief, and wonder, the latter of which we experience when we are overwhelmed by something incomprehensible. Ecstasy is another emotion of joy, as is the sense of achievement after struggling through a tough challenge, a kind of inner pride and joy. There is also a combination of joy and pride that parents experience when their children achieve something great. And, of course, there is the joy-related emotion that isn't quite socially accepted: schadenfreude, where you feel satisfaction when something bad happens to someone else.

Most of these emotions are important for the functioning of our world: struggling to achieve them motivates us to do things that are good for us. We make friends and get curious about new experiences. Positive emotions also encourage us to perform activities that are essential to mankind's survival, like sexual relations and caring for our children. Besides this, many scientists support the theory that people with optimistic outlooks on life actually live longer!

There are obvious differences between a natural and a fake smile. In a real smile, two important muscles are used: *zygomaticus major,* which raises the corners of the mouth, and *orbicularis oculi,* which tenses the area around the eyes. This will cause a bit of a squint, as the skin under the lower eyelid is contracted, the eyebrows are lowered, and lines appear at the sides of the face. Even though we can control zygomaticus major consciously, by raising the corners of our mouth in a smile, the same isn't true of the mus-

Joy: complete expression

"Oh, One Direction is not getting back together after all!"

cle around the eye. Orbicularis oculi is divided into an inner and an outer part. The outer part can only be consciously controlled by 10 percent of all humans. And when it plays no part at all, that makes for a clear and visible difference. When this muscle isn't contracted, we say, "Her mouth is smiling, but her eyes aren't." The fact that we can consciously control orbicularis oculi means, then, both that the smile is incomplete, and therefore revealed as fake, and that it frees up the area around the eyes for other, unconscious signals. In a real smile, the eyebrows are also lowered a little, but nobody who is simulating a smile consciously lowers her eyebrows. Try doing it and you'll see you look a bit frightening.

Some analysis suggests that happily married couples smile and use their eye muscles, while unhappily married couples don't use them. There are also reports of lower blood pressure and more of a feeling of happiness in people who smile a lot with these muscles. It could be that the outer orbicularis oculi needs to be triggered to activate some pleasure centers in the brain, and anybody who only smiles with her mouth would be missing out on this.

We can spot fake smiles incredibly quickly. When I train people to perceive quick changes in facial expressions, I use a sequence of images to simulate microexpressions. One of these images always confuses the people taking the test. The idea is that the microexpression is supposed to represent a happy person. But the person in the photo isn't a great actor, and the joy is only there in the mouth, not in the eyes. Despite the picture being displayed so briefly that the only change you notice consciously is a big smiling mouth, most people get the feeling something's not right. But they have no idea what it is. They don't realize they've just reacted to a dishonest facial expression until later, when they study the picture at their leisure.

So if you want to play it safe when you're faking joy, you have to crack a truly huge smile. Then, almost all the changes the eye muscle takes care of occur just from the width of the smile, since it pushes the cheeks up and makes the skin bunch up under the eyes. This will narrow the eyes and make wrinkles show on the side of them. It makes it a lot more difficult to tell if the smile is genuine or not. The only clue will be the eyebrows and the skin under it, which are lowered by the outer eye muscle in a genuine smile.

Mixed Emotions

To finish off, I want to show you some pictures of mixed emotions, where a face is displaying more than one emotion at once. This is very common in ordinary facial expressions. The trick is to be able to tell which parts come from which emotions, and to be able to do it quickly. The pictures shown on the following page consist of elements from two different emotions. Try to tell which emotions they are, and which parts of the face are expressing them. The answers are on page 124. But try it on your own first without peeking!

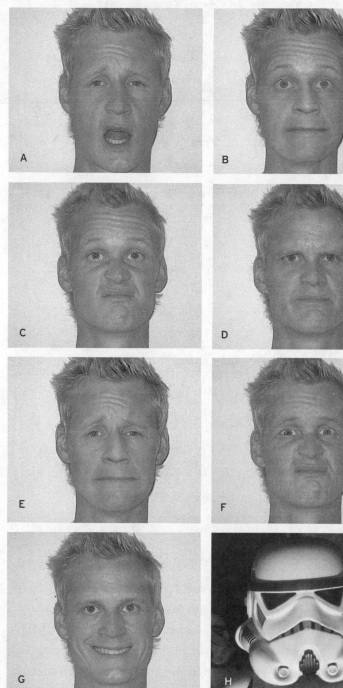

CORRECT ANSWERS

a) Sadness + Anger
   Sadness = eyebrows, eyes. Anger = mouth

b) Surprise + Fear
   Surprise = forehead, eyebrows, eyes. Fear = mouth

c) Disgust + Surprise
   Disgust = mouth, nose, lower eyelids. Surprise = upper eyelids, eyebrows, forehead

d) Anger + Contempt
   Anger = eyebrows, eyes. Contempt = nose, mouth

e) Sadness + Fear
   Sadness = eyebrows, eyes. Fear = mouth

f) Disgust + Fear
   Disgust = mouth, nose, lower eyelids. Fear = upper eyelids, eyebrows, forehead

g) Fake joy
   Joy = mouth. Neutral = the rest of the face

h) Umm . . . Anger? Fear? Desperate for the bathroom? Reptilian? Send your suggestions to the publisher!

ON THE OTHER HAND

As Usual, Things Are More Complicated
Than They Seem

The way I've been describing emotions here, as "labels" for different inherent physical responses, where each emotion (or, at least, each basic emotion) is tied to a specific facial expression, is often referred to as the *classic* view on emotions. Paul Ekman, who I've mentioned a couple times, didn't invent it, but he has been one of the main proponents of this theory in modern times, and has also carried out important research to further our understanding of the field.

However, there are other ways of conceptualizing emotions. Psychology professor Lisa Barrett has recently published results that suggest that the classic view may be incorrect. Many other researchers support her view—in fact, there is a whole movement that's working to change our entire view of emotions.

To begin with, studies measuring the activation of facial muscles have shown that our real-life expressions for the various emotions are not as well-defined as the ones in the pictures that you've just been practicing on. Our faces are constantly in motion, and often, we need to understand the context where an expression occurs in order to be able to determine which emotion it displays. In other words, the pictures you've been studying on these last few pages are simplifications, or stereotypes. The expressions you'll encounter in real life will be much more complex than that.

However, what Barrett is claiming is that not merely our facial expressions, but also what we call our emotions are culturally learned rather than aspects of our biological programming. This is evident from the fact that a single emotion can be expressed in different ways by the body (you may, for example, experience a blood pressure spike on one occasion when you're angry, but not on another), and the same physical expressions can be interpreted as indicating different emotional states depending on their context (profuse sweating can indicate both an upset stomach and being in love).

Therefore, Barrett suggests that instead of talking about emotions, we should talk about emotional categories, in the sense that an emotion within a category can be expressed or experienced in various ways, unlike the classic view, where our emotions are physiologically distinct from one another.

This is called the *constructivist* view, and if it is correct, this whole chapter was a waste of ink. Because within this view, we can't discuss, understand, or detect emotions in the way I've just taught you to.

Although much of the critique Barrett directs at the classic view seems merited to me, I don't find her own view any more convincing. First of all, I'm not sure it's really a problem that our facial expressions for various emotions aren't unique. I've already pointed out that emotional expressions can be very brief, and often contain mixed expressions. But if you're going to learn to tell them apart, we're going to have to begin somewhere. Simplification is a useful, essential technique for learning—we just have to make sure we remember that what we're studying *is* simplified.

Barrett also "proves" the constructivist thesis by making statements such as the following:

There is no single difference between anger and fear, because there's no single "Anger" and no single "Fear" [in bodily terms].

Fear is not a bodily pattern—just as bread is not flour—but emerges from the interactions of [mental] core systems.

The problem here is probably just my own lack of familiarity with scientific jargon, but I still can't see why the fact that the body responds differently in different situations, or that we need mental constructs to fully understand what we're feeling, should contradict any of the things you've learned up to this point. On the other hand, it does complicate things a bit. But human beings are complicated. And things, as usual, are never as simple as they seem.

I'm looking forward to seeing what the next few years will

bring; if Barrett and the constructivists are right, we'll be facing a total paradigm shift when it comes to our understanding of emotions. There are some indications that this is what will happen (and if it does, feel free to tear this chapter out of the book). But let's just say I'm not holding my breath.

Help! I See Emotional People!

How to Respond to Emotions That Are Just Appearing

What should you do when you observe subtle emotional expressions (like the ones you've just learned to recognize) in the person you're talking to? First of all, stay calm. As Charles Darwin wrote in *The Expression of the Emotions in Man and Animals,* "When we witness any deep emotion, our sympathy is so strongly excited, that close observation is forgotten or rendered almost impossible." For any subtle expressions, you never know if the person wants you to know about her emotional state or not. Before you choose to respond to the emotion, you should also determine if what you're seeing is a weak emotion or a strong one that is being controlled. The easiest way to do this is to pay attention to context. If you notice the emotion right at the beginning of a conversation, the source of the emotion probably isn't whatever you're talking about. Then, it's more likely that she brought this emotion with her into the conversation. It may not have anything to do with your relationship and is probably related to something that happened to her earlier. But it could also be about the expectations she has of the conversation or where she thinks it may go.

Most emotional expressions last no longer than a few seconds. How long they last depends on the intensity of the emotion. An intense, short expression that just flashes by is an indication that the emotion is being consciously or unconsciously disguised. A less

intense expression that lasts longer is more often indicative of conscious repression of the emotion. (We're presuming here that she
isn't simply coming out and telling you how she feels.)

There are some emotions you will want to keep from erupting
fully. You should respond to them as soon as you see signs of them,
preferably before she becomes aware of them herself. For other emotions, it's enough to respond to them indirectly and give them some
space in the conversation. What follows are some solid strategies
for responding to each of the different basic emotions we have been
exploring (although I have skipped surprise and joy, since they
rarely need to be "handled").

Sadness

Whether you should respond to somebody's sadness or not depends on your relationship and your previous communication.
Everybody, even your kids, needs some privacy to be able to deal
with the things that upset them, and we all need to be left some
space to withdraw. You can offer a cautious opening for a conversation by asking if everything's OK, but even this depends on the
context and the relationship. The important thing is that if you see
any signs of sadness in somebody, you have to take them seriously.
These signs indicate that something is up and that this person needs
comforting. The only questions are whether it ought to come from
you or from somebody else, and whether it should be now or later.

If there is somebody who is closer to the sad person than you are,
tell the person what you saw. It might be more difficult, because of
the professional relationship, for a manager to comfort an employee
than it would be for one of his colleagues to do so. If it's a close relationship, in your family or your children, you have to make it clear
to whoever is sad that you're there for the person, to talk about it on
his terms, when he wants to.

Anger

When you observe anger in somebody, remember that you probably don't know what caused it or who it is directed at. It isn't necessarily about you. Also, remember that what may look like signs of anger could actually be signs of concentration or confusion. If you're having a conversation, maybe you just haven't explained yourself clearly enough. If you know that the expression is anger, and you want to respond to the emotion, it's a good idea to avoid the word "angry" completely. Maybe he's doing all he can to keep his feelings to himself, and the last thing he needs is for somebody to comment on it. "Whoa, you look angry!" is simply a bad thing to say.

A better idea would be to respond to it at a later time, the day after, perhaps, when emotions aren't running as high and they won't have the same impact on the conversation. If a negotiation or conversation has come to a standstill, and you can't move on because somebody has lost his temper, it's time for a coffee break. Or maybe you could sleep on it instead.

The most effective way of handling somebody's anger and turning it around is to use opinion aikido, which you read about in chapter 3. "If I were in your shoes, I would have reacted in exactly the same way. No doubt about it. Sugar or milk?" If this doesn't work, then you should at least try to make sure nobody makes any decisions or performs any actions that could have consequences further down the road. When we're angry, we tend not to think things through properly.

Fear

If you see somebody display fear, you should begin by reassuring her that she is safe. For example, if you have to give an employee bad news and she starts displaying signs of fear, you should assure her that her job is not in danger or that you are very happy with her efforts. If you've just made somebody uncomfortable, give her a support to lean on so she doesn't fall.

If it's a conversation between close friends, you can be more direct: tell her something seems to be bothering her, and ask if she wants to talk about it. You can also offer security and support by establishing rapport, or use direct physical contact if your relationship is very close. Hugs are always a good way to offer support (assuming they are used the right way; there will be more about this in chapter 10 on anchors), as are their verbal equivalents.

Disgust

Disgust is often mistaken for anger. If somebody starts displaying subtle signs of disgust, like a small wrinkle in the nose, it is probably a sign that the emotion was only just triggered. You should try to respond to it immediately, in a subtle way, without mentioning what you've seen. You could ask if the person felt unfairly treated and if there's something you can do to work it out. Don't get defensive, because that can make the disgust explode completely. You should wait to give your arguments until the other person has finished talking. It's important not to let this one lie and to try to turn this emotional state around at any cost. It's difficult, because the triggers for disgust are deeply embedded within us. But you should remember Gottman's research in the Love Lab—if you can't manage to turn the disgust around, your relationship could be doomed.

Contempt

If somebody shows signs of contempt, it could be indicative of contempt for himself, contempt for whatever you're discussing, or contempt for you as a person. If you suspect it may be directed at you, the best thing to do is actually to leave things be. It could be the good old contempt from inferiority that is sometimes displayed by employees for their bosses, by students for their teachers, and by children for their parents. Or it could be that the person reckons he knows more about what you're discussing and that you're completely wrong.

The person displaying contempt feels he is superior to you. This situation is unfortunately very difficult to turn around, no matter how good you are at establishing rapport. The best thing to do is actually to avoid this person from now on, if possible. If it's a personal relationship, it won't be any good for you anyway. If it's somebody you have to face regularly in work situations or other settings, and whose decisions affect your work, it's best to let somebody else propose your ideas and suggestions in those meetings. You could also see if there is anybody else who holds the same position, somebody you can communicate with directly to get the results you want.

A Little Repetition

You have come a long way on your path as a mind reader. It's time for a break now, to think about all the things you've learned. You've learned to identify a diverse range of signs in unconscious, wordless communication. You've learned to adapt to somebody else's way of communicating within these different areas, to be able to establish a good relationship on cue. You've learned to use this relationship to effect positive change in other people's behavior and attitudes. You've learned to identify different primary senses in different people. You've learned about the differences that the various primary senses make to people's thoughts, speech, and understanding. You've learned to recognize subtle changes in the facial muscles, changes that reveal the various emotional states people are heading into, and how this will alter their experience of your meeting. You've learned how to deflect negative emotions when required.

You've learned all these things. In theory at least.

My suggestion now is for you to go make sure you've learned all of these things in the practical sense, too. Put the book away. Head out into the world to practice mind reading, and keep at it! The second half of this book presumes that you are able to do everything you've read about up to this point. To give you some extra motivation, I will relate a brief story from real life, which should hopefully make it clear to you what a difference knowing how to use these techniques can make.

6

It's Never Too Late

A MORAL TALE ABOUT THE IMPORTANCE
OF READING MINDS

*An interlude in which I tell you what can happen
when you use—or don't use—your mind-reading skills.*

A year or so ago, I was the emcee at a one-day conference. Several different seminars were taking place at once, all with different schedules, so there was a lot to do and I was soon very busy. I arrived at lunch quite a bit later than the other participants. I noticed a man who was sitting alone, still eating, and sat down with him. As I sat down I began to tell him about a funny incident that had occurred earlier in the day. I broke off abruptly when I saw the man's reaction: he was staring at me with an expression of extreme disapproval. I felt like an insect under his gaze. I could have let it go right there and eaten my lunch in silence, but I wasn't just the emcee—I was going to be performing later that evening. And I thought it would be a bad idea for me to let any of the audience members turn against me this early in the day.

I realized that I had committed a cardinal sin by not paying attention to who was actually sitting at that table, not proper attention. I had just gone ahead and started talking about myself without bothering to find out whom I was talking to. Now that I took a look at the man, I could see that he had all the classic attributes of kinesthesia: he was powerfully built, wearing a flannel shirt, and even had a beard. The fact that he was sitting and eating on his own supported my observation, because I estimated that it was because he ate slower than the others, at the pace of a kinesthetic. And there I had been, rushing in to try to interest him in an extremely visual anecdote. It wasn't any real surprise that things had gone wrong.

So I sat there eating my food for a few minutes, while I began establishing rapport by following his body language and tempo (which was, predictably enough, much slower than mine). When I noticed that the lowered, contracted eyebrows he had displayed when he stared at me had gone away, I asked him a few control questions to see if he really was kinesthetic, while my voice followed the tempo of his movements. I asked if he was enjoying his food and what he thought about the conference. After that, I repeated the same story again. But this time I made an effort to use a different range of words when I told it and to accentuate the elements I suspected he would find the most important. I no longer described the beautiful curve an object had followed as it sailed through the air. On the other hand, I put great weight on how it felt when the object made impact with the back of my head. Yes, I know—it shouldn't make any difference, according to the research we discussed earlier. But I did it anyway. This time the story was a success. By the end of our lunch, we were getting on very well.

This must have looked very odd to anyone looking on, because superficially there was no great difference. The first time I told him something, I was met with an angry glare. A short while later I repeated the same thing and was rewarded with approval instead.

I had used my knowledge of rapport, sensory impressions, and subtle expressions of emotion to change an uncomfortable situation

into a good relationship, in just a few seconds. I just stopped thinking about myself and paid attention to the other guy for a while. It's
never too late to establish some rapport, not even when things have
started off on the wrong foot. This was fortunate, because it turned
out that the man I had met was the managing director of the company that had hired me for the day.

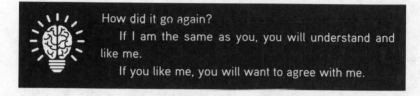

How did it go again?
   If I am the same as you, you will understand and
like me.
   If you like me, you will want to agree with me.

7

Be a Human Lie Detector

CONTRADICTORY SIGNS AND WHAT THEY MEAN

In which you learn to recognize signs of pressure in people, and a student gives us the finger.

I n this chapter and in the next, I want to discuss two special cases of "practical wordless communication." There are some unconscious signs that we only display in certain situations. For instance, chapter 8 will be about attraction. You'll be amazed at what your unconscious mind gets up to when it believes it has found a suitable match for your genes (i.e., an interesting hottie). But before then, we'll take a look at a different interesting topic—the changes that can be seen in our wordless communication when we try to lie to someone.

As a mind reader it is important, naturally, to be able to tell when somebody is lying to you. You've already learned to identify a certain kind of false sign, since you learned to tell a faked facial expression from a genuine one. However, as you'll see, when it comes to lies, we've barely scratched the surface.

The easiest way for us to lie is with our words, since that is what we've been practicing all of our lives. We are a little less good at lying with our facial expressions, although we've had a bit of practice in this area, too. The thing we're the worst at is lying with our bodies. Most of us probably haven't even thought of the fact that our bodies actually "speak" a lot. So it's ironic that we pay the most attention to what somebody is saying to us, and give that person's facial expression less weight.

If we suspect that somebody might be lying to us, we will concentrate even more on what is being said—when we ought to be doing the opposite. If we want to know what somebody is really telling us, we should care less about the words that are spoken and more about whatever he is expressing with the rest of his body and with his tone of voice.

But can you actually tell when somebody's lying? Yes. And no. We can detect certain signs that are displayed for a certain kind of lie, which involves a certain level of emotional stress. So what we will usually see is that somebody is stressed or nervous, rather than that he is lying per se. But sometimes these signs are all we need to deduce that somebody is telling untruths. There are also some signs that only appear when somebody is lying. The trick is finding them.

Some people are very good at telling when somebody is trying to fool them with a lie, and others never learn to do it. And, of course, some people are born liars and don't show any leakage at all (the best ones tend to be psychopaths), while others can't even lie about how many donuts they've eaten without giving themselves away. We're all different, but most of us display several of these signs, and most of us can improve our skills at identifying them.

What Is a Lie?

The art of lie detection fascinates many people, especially those of us that work in the police, military, and courts. Since the classic

lie-detector machine, the polygraph, is often unreliable,* people con-
ducting research into lies (one of whom is Paul Ekman, mentioned
earlier) have spent a lot of effort on identifying the signs that could
reveal a lie. They've made some good progress. But what do we
really mean when we use the word "lie"?

Most of us lie all the time, in the sense that what we say doesn't
accurately represent the true state of affairs. Our social rules pre-
suppose a large number of trivial lies. If we're asked, "How are you
doing?" we'll often answer, "Fine, thanks, and you?" even when we
feel anything but fine. We know that the person who asked the
question isn't actually interested in a detailed description of our
state and is simply using it as a phrase of greeting.

In some situations, we're expected to lie and display something
other than our true feelings. In a beauty pageant, it's OK for the
winner to cry and be emotional, while the runners up have to show
how happy they are for the winner and be strong about their loss.
If they would all show how they really felt, we'd probably get to see
the finalists in tears and the winner shrieking with laughter and
happiness. To hide your emotions, or to pretend to feel something
other than what you really do feel, is another form of lying.

Of course, we're not interested in these kinds of permissible lies.
The kind of lies that interest us occur when somebody lies in a
context that isn't socially or culturally permitted and when the mo-
tive for lying is personal gain. This also means that the lie has to be
a conscious one, so the liar has to know that what she is saying
doesn't correctly describe reality. Remember, a lie can be a claim,
but it can also be a matter of which emotions we display or don't. If

---

* Polygraphs aren't necessarily unreliable. The problem is you always need somebody to sit
there afterward and interpret the results. And that's where things can go wrong, because
any interpretation is just that—a personal opinion. A polygraph is great at being "the machine that goes *ping*." The problem is figuring out what this *ping* is supposed to mean.

I tell you I won a tennis match that I actually lost, I'm lying to you. But if I display happiness in my actions and with my facial expression when I am really sad, I'm lying, too.

When somebody lies, there's always a reward and/or a punishment involved, which is the reason for the lie. You lie to get a reward you wouldn't get otherwise, or to avoid a punishment you're about to be given. It could also be a combination of these: you lie to get a reward you're not really entitled to, somebody's appreciation for instance, but if the lie is discovered, you could be punished for it when the other person ends the relationship.

Contradictory Signs

The detectable signs of a lie are displayed when the reward or punishment involved isn't trivial, so there is actually something at stake for the person lying, and she really cares if her lie is successful or not. Then the person trying to lie will also be emotionally invested in the lie, and it's this commitment to the lie that gives rise to many of the signs a mind reader will be looking for. Identifying the signs is one thing, but then the problem of knowing what they mean still remains.

In any lie, there are two competing messages: the truth and the falsehood. The word "lie" focuses on the falsehood, but both are actually just as important. The ability to tell them apart is important, too. Since we are always giving off different messages in all of our communications, not just with our words, a lie is actually a more-or-less-successful attempt at controlling these messages. Just as can be the case with some facial expressions, a lie is an attempt at covering up or masking a certain message beneath another one. Being able to tell when somebody's lying is a matter of paying attention to the elements of our communication that we're not so good at controlling. A person who tells the truth expresses the same thing with her consciously controlled communication as she does with her unconscious expressions. But if we can detect some disharmony in what is expressed, between what the hands and the words are communicating, for instance, we may suspect that there are two different messages involved. We look for *contradictory signs,* unconscious signs that say something other than the consciously expressed message. The signs that are difficult for us to control express our true thoughts and feelings.

Evolutionary psychologist Robert Trivers has a solution to this problem for those who want to be able to lie freely. The trick is simply to convince yourself that your lie is true! Then, all the signs, conscious as well as unconscious, will genuinely be expressing a single message. It won't catch up with you until it's time to eat that last cookie you hid and swore you'd never stolen—since you no longer believe you took it.

The unconscious, contradictory signs a liar displays are called *leakage.* When somebody lies, or tries to keep feelings from us, there will be leakage in a number of different areas. But you have to be careful: some people don't display any leakage at all, however much they lie. So you can't interpret a lack of leakages as a guarantee that somebody is telling the truth. There are also some people who we believe are displaying leakage but who are actually just behaving normally. Because of this, it's important to know that the signs you do detect are *changes* in somebody's behavior, not just the way she always behaves. You should make a point of noticing several different kinds of leakage in somebody before deciding that she is or isn't lying or holding back her emotions.

Once you've observed a number of contradictory signs in somebody, that could mean that he's lying to you, but it could also mean that he actually feels some other emotion than the one he is trying to display. Often you won't have any problems deciding what the situation is. The context in which the signs are observed make it clear to you.

You should also remember that even though you've noticed several of these signs, you don't necessarily know what caused them. As you will soon see, they can be caused by completely different things other than the fact that the person is lying. You might see lots of leakage in somebody, but they could be due to something he just thought of that has nothing to do with your conversation. When you discover these signs in somebody, your next step is to consider the context and any other possible reasons there could be for the behavior, before you can confidently say that somebody is lying.

Why Are You Scratching Your Nose?

Contradictory Signs in Body Language

The most obvious of all of these contradictory signs is given by the body's own autonomic nervous system. We have no ability to control it, even if we discover we are displaying signs through it. It's very difficult, if not impossible, to stop sweating or blushing on cue, or to avoid having your pupils dilate when you get a winning hand at the poker table. The problem is that the autonomic nervous system is only activated when the emotions are very strong. Fortunately, there are loads of other signs and leakage, which appear even when the emotions aren't so strong.

The Face

It is often said that a face carries two messages: what we want to project and what we actually think. Sometimes they are one and the same, but they often aren't. When we try to control the message we project, we do it in three ways:

- **Qualification** We comment on the facial expression we have by adding another one to it. For instance, adding a smile to an otherwise miserable expression to show everybody that we'll pull through.
- **Modulate** We change the intensity of the expression to weaken or strengthen it. We do this by controlling the number of muscles involved (as we do when we display a *partial* facial expression), how much we use those muscles (as we do when we display a complete but low-intensity, that is, a *slight,* expression), and for how long we display the expression.
- **Falsification** We can display an emotion when we're not actually feeling anything (*simulation*). We can attempt to not reveal anything when we're actually feeling something (*neutralization*). Or we can cover up the emotion we're feeling with another emotion that we aren't feeling (*masking*).

To be able to pretend to have an emotion in a convincing way, we need to know how to express it, that is, which muscles to use, and how to use them. Children and adolescents practice this by making faces in front of the mirror, but we tend to stop doing this as we grow older. For this reason, we sometimes have a bad idea of how we actually look when we're expressing various things. Often we won't have time to prepare, either, and will have to base the look on how it feels inside, and hope we'll get close enough.

Neutralizing, not displaying anything at all, is very difficult, especially when it's about something we care about, which provokes a strong emotion in us that we want to keep hidden. This will often stiffen us up to the point where it's obvious we're hiding something, even if nobody can tell what we're hiding. So we prefer to take the easier way out and mask it, pretending to feel something other than our genuine emotion. When we try to control our facial expressions, we tend to only use the lower portion of our faces, as you should know by now. This means that the area around the eyes, eyebrows, and forehead is free to display our true emotions, something we do unconsciously. For even when we make an effort to smile, the nose can wrinkle up in disgust over something. You've just read the chapter about emotions and learned what the signs displayed by our eyes, eyebrows, and forehead signify, no matter what we try to express with our mouths, so I won't repeat that here.

The most commonly used mask to hide our emotions is a smile. Darwin, who wrote one of the seminal works on facial muscles and body language, offers a theory as to why this is. He claimed that we usually try to mask negative emotions, and that the use of muscles in smiling is the furthest removed from negative expressions.

On pages 120–121, I showed you how to tell the difference between a fake smile and a genuine one. A genuine smile is always symmetrical: both corners of the mouth are raised equally as much; it can never be asymmetrical (assuming the person doesn't suffer from some facial-muscle injury). A fake smile can be either symmetrical or asymmetrical, and so it can occur solely on one side of the face. If you observe a crooked smile, it's therefore either a failed attempt at looking happy or actually a part of a different expression, like disgust or contempt. It also uses both the outer and inner part of the area around the eyes, which is almost impossible to do consciously.

Actors that are able to make a natural smile, including the eyes, usually do it by bringing to mind a positive memory, making them genuinely happy. Fake expressions of joy are also often given away by bad timing. They are assembled a little too quickly. A genuine expression of joy can take some time to be completed, and a fake one tends to also be displayed for too long.

Microexpressions can also appear in these situations. Personally, I think microexpressions play a huge part in our hunches about people. If we feel that somebody doesn't like us, despite the person being nothing but polite on the surface, it is probable that our hunch was caused by body language and other unconscious communication that we've picked up on. But there is also some likelihood that we've noticed a microexpression that has told us what the person really feels about us. It may have been too quick for us to notice consciously, but our unconscious mind has plenty of time to register it.

Microexpressions are reliable leakage whenever they appear. However, some people don't display them at all, while others do in some situations, but not in others, and so on. Not seeing any microexpressions in somebody is no guarantee that she isn't trying to suppress an emotion, if that's what you suspect. In that case, you'll have to look for signs elsewhere.

The Eyes

It is commonly believed that you can tell when somebody is lying by observing the eyes. We think we know that shifty eyes, frequent blinking, and whether or not somebody looks us in the eyes is a sign that that person is lying. This isn't necessarily wrong, but since everybody has heard of these things, it will often be the case that somebody who's lying will actually look you in the eyes more than he would otherwise! Since most of us have been told that a liar won't dare to make eye contact, a liar is likely to overcompensate instead.

There are some moods that cause our eyes to be averted in a natural way. We look down when we're sad; we slant our heads down or lean them away when we feel shame or guilt; and we bluntly look away when we disapprove of somebody. A liar won't do this, for fear of being exposed as a liar(!). The best liars avoid detection by knowing exactly when to turn their eyes away.

Another factor that has to do with the eyes is the size of the pupils. As I mentioned earlier, the pupils dilate when we feel emotions like appreciation or interest. Try to make sure that the size of the pupils matches the emotions that the person in question is claiming to feel. Somebody who is taking an active interest in something shouldn't have pinpoint pupils, unless the sun is right in her eyes.

When somebody who is lying or under emotional pressure blinks, the eyes will often remain closed for longer than they do with somebody who is telling the truth. Zoologist Desmond Morris, who has also studied human behavior, has observed this phenomenon in police interrogations and claims that it is an unconscious attempt at shutting the world out.

How we move our eyes can also provide clues to the thoughts that go through our minds. We often use our memories when we think, but we are also capable of constructing new events, which we have never experienced, with our imaginations. This is what happens when we're being creative, planning our futures, making up stories, and so on. Do you remember the EAC model for eye motions and sensory impressions? Check it out on pages 63–64 if you've forgotten it. It tells us that our eyes will make different motions depending on whether we are constructing a thought or remembering something. We're constantly constructing thoughts, and sometimes constructing means we're lying. If someone tells you about something she claims to have done or experienced, but her eyes suddenly go to the place they usually go when she is being creative, this would indicate that she is constructing a thought. You will need to ask yourself if there is any reason for this person to be using her creativity and imagination in that context. For example, if she says, "I had to work late, and since I would have been late for dinner anyway, I grabbed a pizza and a beer with Josh, but then I came straight home" and you observe a construction occurring when she says, "I grabbed a pizza and a beer with Josh," it's time for caution. There is obviously some kind of problem with this claim. It *could* be that you are the victim of a straight-up lie.

Maybe this is the reason for the cliché about liars being afraid of eye contact. According to those who put faith in the EAC model, the eyes are moved when a lie is constructed, which will make it difficult for the liar to retain eye contact, as that would require him to look straight ahead. On the other hand, telling somebody about a memory you have while looking straight ahead (and maintaining eye contact) will usually work, since this eye position allows for visualizing previous memories.

Remember, the EAC model will only work as a lie detector if you can catch somebody in the act of constructing a lie as it is uttered. If somebody has had time to prepare for his lie, that is, construct it in advance, you may not see any difference, since the lie has become a *memory,* even though its content is still imaginary. And finally, let me remind you again that this model isn't a general truth. There are plenty of exceptions to it, so before you make somebody sleep on the couch, make sure you can truly tell the difference in their particular behavior between remembering and construction.

CONSTRUCTION EXERCISE

Even if the EAC model doesn't apply fully to everyone, most people still make *some* personal change in their behaviors or eye motions that indicate that they are mentally constructing an idea. You can perform the following exercise to improve your ability to spot somebody making a visual construction:

Step 1: Ask the person to visualize something, like in the earlier exercise with the *Mona Lisa*. Give her plenty of time to paint the full picture in her mind, which will also give you an opportunity to observe her eye motions.

Step 2: Now ask the person to imagine a new version of this image, one that doesn't exist. *Mona Lisa* as painted by a five-year-old, for example. Again, give her enough time to get into this task and construct the image in as detailed a way as possible. In the meantime, you can observe if she follows the EAC model or not and see if you can find any other signs of construction.

Step 3: Feel free to do the exercise again to make sure the changes you observed are part of her consistent behavior and not freak events. (But remember to use a different picture the second time! Otherwise, there won't be any construction in step 2, as she can simply remember her previously constructed memory.)

Hands

The farther away from the face we get, the easier it is for us to lie with our wordless signs, since the rest of our body isn't as strongly connected to the emotional centers in our brain, and is under our control to a greater degree. So it's a good thing we forget to do it, lie with them, that is. The hands are somewhere in between; we are quite aware of them, as we can see our hands most of the time, but they also provide a huge number of unconscious signs.

Desmond Morris refers to certain kinds of hand gestures as *emblems*. They work in exactly the same way words do: they are specific gestures, with specific meanings, known to all members of a certain culture. An example of this is the gesture Winston Churchill introduced, where the index and middle fingers are extended and the palm is turned forward. In most of the Western world, this is recognized as the sign "V for victory." Lying with this kind of gesture is no problem, of course. There is no trouble at all making the victory sign when somebody asks you if your team won a game you actually lost big.

But sometimes we use these kinds of gestures unconsciously, in a kind of body language equivalent to a Freudian slip. When this kind of gesture appears as an unconscious slip, it is a good indicator of the true feelings somebody holds, for the simple reason that it is unconscious. These gestures can be hard to notice, though, as they will often be made in unusual body positions compared to how they are ordinarily used. An example of this is the gesture Paul Ekman discovered when he arranged for a number of students to be interviewed by an extremely unsympathetic professor. The unconscious gesture he discovered in several cases was a fist with an extended middle finger. The proverbial bird. But instead of being a conscious action, with a raised fist, the hand was rested on the knee, with the finger pointing to the floor. There was no doubt that this was a sign of strong dislike, despite the fact that the person who made the gesture was completely unaware of having made it.

Another common unconscious gesture is the shrug, which we make consciously to show that we don't know, have an opinion about, or care about something. But instead of pulling up your shoulders, raising your hands, and turning the palms out at chest level, like you would ordinarily do it, the unconscious shrug is made with straight arms that hang down. The shoulder motion is left out or minimal, and the traces of the emblem that we see are the hands turning up or out at waist level.

Other kinds of hand motions are the ones we use to clarify what we're talking about or to illustrate an abstract concept. Like when we draw a square in the air with our finger and say "it was completely square." Almost everybody uses their hands when they speak, even though cultural and personal factors determine the frequency and intensity of such gestures. Scandinavians don't use their hands much when they speak, and the Italians are the unrivaled masters of hand gestures. But just about everybody uses their hands to some degree, and we're actually very dependent on this kind of gesture to understand others, even though we rarely note people's hand gestures consciously.

It's impossible to communicate with somebody who illustrates her words with the wrong hand gestures. When I give classes, I often illustrate this by making eye contact with somebody and asking the person what the time is while pointing at the window with my hand. The answer is invariably "Uhhh . . . huh?" even though the actual literal question is so simple to answer. But there are occasions when our use of hand gestures is minimal: when we are very tired, or very sad, or very bored, or when we really, really need to think about what we're saying. And when we consider. Our. Every. Word. Carefully. Like when we lie.

Constructing new thoughts is a demanding internal process. When we need to focus on it, our external expressions will be subdued. Hand gestures are very distinctive expressions, and their absence is always obvious.

When I ask how we can tell if somebody is lying, there's always somebody who mentions that liars scratch their noses. It's actually true that hand gestures toward the face increase when you lie, but the most common one actually isn't scratching your nose. That's in second place. The most common gesture is covering your mouth, as if to stop the lie from getting out, or as if you were ashamed of what you're about to say. It is likely that all the other hand gestures to the face—adjusting your glasses, tugging at your earlobe, scratching your nose—are actually the same basic gesture that has been deflected from the mouth, to do something less-suspect instead.

You can also see this kind of hand motion in people who are simply listening to somebody. We often cover our own mouth when we're doubtful of something we're being told, or when we don't think we're being told the truth. It's easy to imagine a surprised person thinking "I can't believe it!" with wide eyes, and covering her mouth with her hand. If you observe this behavior in somebody, it's time to make an effort to be clearer and confirm the truth of what you're saying. If you're telling the truth, that is. If you're not, you might get an itchy nose. . . .

Just like all the other signs of lying, the fact that somebody is scratching her nose doesn't necessarily indicate anything more than an itchy nose. But if it happens repeatedly, it might be a good idea to start looking for other signs of lies or concealed emotions.

The Rest of the Body

Other things you might want to pay attention to are posture, legs, and feet. An interested person's posture will make an alert impression, of course, while an uninterested person can't help but shrink away a little. If it goes on for long enough, we may end up leaning against a wall or the edge of a table, until we realize how bored we look, and try to change things by coughing and adjusting our posture in a very obvious way.

We're terrible at keeping track of which signals we're giving off with our legs and feet. This is probably because we spend so much time with our legs hidden under tables and because we've learned to only look at people's faces and ignore the rest.

A classic example of contradictory signs would be a travel agent who's just spent forty minutes selling a nine-hundred-dollar holiday package to a young couple in love, but has been thinking about all the other holidays he could have sold for more money if he hadn't been tied up with these kids. He is unconsciously kicking his foot toward them under the table, an obviously aggressive signal. Or another example would be the shy girl at a speed-dating session who's trying to seem relaxed but has one leg wrapped tightly around the other underneath the table.

Gestural Slips

Lots of situations can cause nervous tension or stress. Sometimes it's natural, like when we're going for an important job interview, giving a speech at some big party, feeling really bored and restless, about to have our first child, starting school, or something like that. We call it "butterflies in the stomach."

Something else that can also cause nervous tension, stress, and anxiety is lying about something that's important. When we're in this situation, we're carrying around a lot of energy and anxiety, which has to find some release. If we try to not show anything at all and just focus on being completely cool, we'll eventually start shaking. We could even faint if we tense up like that. So it's better to keep busy doing something. There is a certain kind of action that is like a release system for anxiety and nerves: *gestural slips.*

This kind of action is a clear sign that somebody has a lot of internal conflict or tension going on. Gestural slips are small, repetitive, and meaningless actions. For example, constantly clicking a ballpoint pen, tearing paper into small pieces, or tapping your fingers. Some research indicates that we have a great need to keep our hands constantly occupied, so it can sometimes be hard to determine if the behavior you're observing in somebody is a gestural slip or not. So it's important to confirm that it's a recurring, repeated (looped) action.

Somebody who has found a good gestural slip with which to keep herself busy can seem as cool as a cucumber in every other respect. She may not even know why she just sorted all the toothpicks in the jar. But you can tell that it's a sign of heavy internal stress. What you need to find out is if it is warranted or not.

Airports all over the world have staff that walk around looking for these very signs in travelers, to identify people who are afraid of flying but trying to hide it, since they could cause a problem once they're on the plane. They're often in the smoking lounge or, if there isn't one, outside the terminal. (And since 9/11, nervous flyers have taken on a completely different dimension in a lot of countries.) The guy in the suit who knocks the ash off of his cigarette more often than he really needs to is one example. The sophisticated lady breaking all of the matches one by one before disposing of them in the ashtray is another. Smoking itself is, of course, sometimes a very obvious gestural slip, if it seems to happen mechanically, smoke after smoke, instead of being a short moment of pleasure for the smoker. In a conversation with me, the public relations officer at Arlanda Airport in Stockholm confirmed that the customs and security staff are also trained to be observant of these signals.

Remember, gestural slips can be completely natural. There are lots of situations in which we have a lot of energy that we can't find any suitable release for, and it "sneaks out" in meaningless activities like tapping your fingers, biting your nails, or messing around with lit candles. There are also times in our lives when we're constantly overcharged with more energy or frustration than we can release. Take a look at how a teenager exhibits gestural slips if she has to sit still for more than a fraction of a second.

You Sound Nervous; Is Something Up?

Changes in the Voice

Even though it's easy for us to choose which words we want to use when we speak, we have a harder time controlling our actual voices. Our emotional states affect how we sound. And, actually, we're not as good at choosing the words as we think, either.

Tone of Voice

As you have no doubt noticed, your voice often gets higher when you're angry. The tone changes. The volume increases, too, as well as the tempo. When you're sad, the opposite will happen. Your voice will come from the back of your throat and be deeper. You will speak slowly and a lot more quietly than otherwise.

There are some indications that our voices are affected the same way when we're feeling guilty about lying as they are when we're angry. We start speaking quicker, higher, and louder. If we're feeling ashamed of having to lie, instead of guilty, our voices will be affected the same way they are when we're sad. We become quieter, our voices lower, and our speech slows down. If this is true, it means that if you observe these changes to somebody's voice, and there's no reasonable reason why she should suddenly have become angry or sad, you may need to consider the possibility that she's lying to you.

Changes in Speech

When we're lying, the way we speak changes, as well as the quality of our voices. Pauses will start appearing in our speech, for instance. We start using pauses that are too long or too short, compared to our previous speech patterns. We suddenly pause where we normally wouldn't, like in mid-sentence. Or before we answer questions we ought to know the answer to immediately. We try to buy time by lengthening our vowels, making noises like "Ehhhhh . . ." or "Uuhhhhhh . . ." while we desperately think of something to say. Nerves can make stutters appear suddenly in people who otherwise don't stutter.

We use repetition and say the same thing in the same way, over and over. We use repetition and say the same thing in the same way, over and over. This has to do with the fact that we suddenly like to speak in long sentences, as if we were afraid of what could happen if we let somebody else get a word in, so we start speaking in long, endless sentences with no end. An easy way to do that is to use repetition, because that way you can keep going on forever, saying the same thing over and over again without anybody else getting a word in.

Or we do the opposite. Suddenly. Begin. To. Speak. In. Very. Short. Sentences. As though we. Were afraid. Of slipping up. Of saying too much.

All of these kinds of changes in somebody's speech are a serious warning that there is something going on. At this point, you should start looking for other indications in the face or body language.

Changes in Language

People who lie often exhibit a number of linguistic peculiarities. They begin to say things in ways they would never speak otherwise. Many of these linguistic peculiarities are so well known by now that they have become clichés, so common that we suspect a lie as soon as we hear them. They can even seem transparent to the liar himself, but that doesn't make it any easier for him to avoid using them. Many of these language changes get past most people's lie-detecting skills. So it's a good idea to learn to listen for them. Behavioral psychologist Peter Collett has identified the following:

- **Digressions and Vagaries** Liars will often digress more and give complicated explanations that don't seem to be going anywhere: *"Well, I guess you could say that, well, I mean, it could be, yeah, I mean sure. . . ."*

  Direct questions will get short answers, however.

- **The Same Thing Every Time** Lies are often told without too much detail. And if you ask the same question later, the liar will probably repeat exactly what he said before. Somebody who's telling the truth is more likely to include new information or shorten parts of what you were told earlier. Memories aren't something we take out of some box in our mind every time we want to look at them, then put back the same. Our memories are affected by everything else that goes on in our minds at the time we talk about them.

  Somebody who isn't lying is therefore able to focus on different things each time she tells somebody about something, while a liar always says the same thing, out of fear of self-contradiction, and seldom goes into detail. If you ask somebody who's telling the truth to give you more detail about something than she did before, she can do it (unless the memory is so old she's lost the details). But for a liar, this is impossible, unless she constructs a new lie on the spot. It goes something like this:

"I was on my own all night. I watched TV, and then I went to bed."

"What did you watch?"

"Uhhh . . . Let's see . . . It was, umm . . ."

- **Smoke Screens** A liar will often try to protect himself behind a protective layer of impressive empty words, like using abstractions excessively, which I'll tell you more about in a while, or pure *non sequiturs*. Liars will often respond in ways that are meant to sound like they make sense but actually don't. Collett points out that this is what David Dinkins, ex-mayor of New York, did when he was accused of tax fraud: "I haven't committed a crime. What I did was fail to comply with the law." Duh.

  Example: *"I could answer that question both ways, depending on how you put it."*

- **Creating Distance with Denial** A liar will tend to speak in terms of negatives. He will start to define things in terms of what they're *not* rather than in terms of what they *are*, which would otherwise be the normal way for us to talk. A good example is Nixon's famous statement: "I am not a crook." It would have been natural to say, "I am an honest man." He was so aware of, so focused on what he was denying, that he formulated his lie completely around it.

  Example: *"I'm not lying"* (as opposed to *"I'm telling the truth"*).

- **Creating Distance with Depersonalization** Liars avoid using words like "me" or "mine" as much as possible. This is a way of distancing themselves from the lie. For the same reason, liars will also tend to use generalizations like "always," "never," "everybody," "nobody," and so on, to evade having to define exactly who or what they're talking about.

Example: *"You can relax. That kind of thing never happens around here."*

- **Creating Distance Using Past Tense** Another way of distancing oneself from whatever one is lying about is to relocate the lie to another time and express the content of the lie in the past tense rather than the present tense. An example of this is the common answer to the question, "What *are* you doing?!" A liar would answer, *"I wasn't doing anything!"* (as opposed to *"I'm not doing anything"*).

- **Expressing Reservations** A lot of bad lies in movies begin with the words "Listen, I know you won't believe this, but . . ." or "I know this sounds strange, but . . ." A liar who realizes she is straining credulity will often use these kinds of reservations. In this way, she confirms any suspicions the other person may have but simultaneously explains that they're unnecessary. The problem is that this is such a common way of shielding a lie. The simple fact that somebody expresses reservations about what she's about to say will often make us doubt whatever she then proceeds to say. The funniest kind of reservation is when we actually tell the person it's a lie straight out, without even knowing it.

Example: *"I tell you, it was unreal! Let me tell you what happened. . . ."*

- **Linguistic Sophistication** It's a little strange, but people who are lying will often use stricter forms of speech than they otherwise would. Many will often suddenly begin to follow rules of grammar and pronunciation that they otherwise don't obey, and will leave out favorite slang expressions and informal abbreviations. Collett claims that this is because these people are tense and so behave in a more formal fashion. I think it may also have to do with the fact that they unconsciously want to emphasize what they're saying and get it all as right as they can. This is really about the content of the lie, but it spills over into how they deliver the lie. The lack of truth in the lie is overcompensated for by being on their best behavior in the linguistic sense. If we secretly don't care about something either way, but want to pretend we care, we won't settle for a simple "No, that doesn't sound good"; we would rather use something like:

"I feel that would be both regrettable and inappropriate."

- **Drawing Your Words Ooooouut** A lie takes time to formulate, hence all of the vocal changes are used, like pauses, stutters, drawn-out vowels, and so on. This can also cause the lie to be told at a slower tempo than at which the liar would usually speak, at least initially:

    "Yeaaah, iiiiiit's liiiiiiiike thiiiiiis—sorry—waaaaaas liiiiike thiiiiis. . . ." (Note the distancing in the change between "is" and "was"!)

A Word of Caution

Be Careful About Your Conclusions

Before I end this chapter, I'd like to repeat some important things that a mind reader needs to think about when trying to tell if people are lying (or trying to hide their true emotions). Remember, spotting one of these signs isn't enough. All a sign means is that you should keep a lookout for more of them. The signs also have to be changes in somebody's behavior. If they were there to begin with, you can't determine if they are caused by the person lying or if they're just part of her natural behavior.

You should also remember that the signs you will be spotting won't tell you if it is a (spoken) lie or a case of repressed emotions. You will need the context to determine that. Just as with masked emotions, these signs can also be caused by something that has nothing to do with the context you're involved in. If you were talking to that businessman who was afraid of flying, you'd be making a mistake if you assumed his displays of gestural slips were a sign that he was lying to you (unless you were talking about flying, of course).

If you're picking up clear signs that something isn't right, proceed with caution. Give the other person an opportunity to change or add to her statement. Don't say, "AHA! Caught you lying!" Instead, say something like, "I feel like there's something else you're feeling about all this, something you haven't told me." Or, "Would you mind clarifying what you've been saying? Maybe there's something you'd like to explain differently, to help me understand better."

Remember your opinion aikido. If you confront a suspected liar directly and accuse her of lying, you will most likely get nothing back but resistance and denial. Show some understanding, establish some rapport. Find out what's really going on. And finally, if you're not sure, you should always presume the person is being truthful.

It's obviously not very constructive to go around suspecting everyone of lying to you. The things you've just learned are good skills to have, but you'll have a nicer life if you assume you won't need to use them. And something that can make life very, very nice is to find a nice *person* to share some of it (life, that is) with. Which we actually do. All the time. Unfortunately, we are often so bad at consciously reading signs of interest from other people (and they are no better) that we keep missing each other all the time. The next chapter will help you change that.

Some people exhibit more or less every single classical sign of lying in their natural behavior. I know a guy like that, and he had a terrible time with his girlfriend until she got the hang of it.

Remember, you have to know how somebody acts normally before you can determine what constitutes a change in his or her behavior.

8

The Unconscious Pickup Artist

HOW YOU FLIRT WITH PEOPLE
WITHOUT EVEN KNOWING IT

*In which your ears will blush when you realize
how shameless your own behavior is during coffee breaks,
and you get a trip to the Caribbean as a reward.*

I t's obvious, really: one of the areas in which being able to read the body language of others and control your own is the most useful is when we find ourselves attracted to or otherwise interested in somebody. There is an entire library of wordless, unconscious communication that we can dip into when our unconscious mind gets into the mood. Perhaps this is making you feel guilty, and you think "But I have a boyfriend" or "There's no point in my reading this; I'm happily married." Your marital status is, however, completely irrelevant. Human beings are social animals. We require acknowledgment from others—and to be permitted to acknowledge other members of our pack—to be able to feel good. Just as is the case with emotions, this is an important mechanism for the functioning of our social structures and for our capacity to enjoy our lives. Flirting, a little bit of acknowledgment, can be a very small and very innocent thing. Of course, it could ultimately lead to procreation and the furthering of the species, but in its initial stages, it's really just a more specifically directed kind of rapport, which is also a kind of acknowledgment.

Also, I personally believe that those who live in steady relationships might be especially in need of putting a bit of flirtation back into their lives, to spice their relationships up. And besides, even if you don't have any desire to flirt with anyone but your partner, it might be nice to get a boost of confidence from knowing that somebody is interested in you, just by looking at him or her. Or if you're not in a relationship, how do you reveal your own interest without being too obvious about it? Or if that exciting person comes over to talk to you, how do you keep him interested so he doesn't just walk away and disappear? And what's the best way to reject somebody?

I'm aware of flirting classes in which they teach things like "caressing somebody with your eyes" and doing a lot of licking the lips, but that's not quite what I want to talk about. This is, rather, about all the things we actually already do, unconsciously and wordlessly. Let's have a look at how we go about it!

Rapport and Eye Contact*

Imagine you're in some kind of social space. There are lots of other people there. Maybe it's a Christmas party at work, a movie premiere, or a wedding. It could also be a waiting room at a train station, an area where you are picking your kids up at day care, or in the lunchroom at work. Imagine that you're there with some friends

---

* What you're about to read is true of both men and women. We usually use the same methods when we're flirting. On the occasions where the methods are different, I will point this out.

and talking to them. Suddenly, your unconscious mind sees somebody a few feet away to your right, somebody you unconsciously find exciting. The first thing you do is to establish rapport with this person from across the room or area. Do you remember the rapport exercise, earlier in the book? You begin adapting to the other person's body language and tempo. You also make sure to keep your body "open" to the other person, removing any obstacles like a drinking glass, bicycle helmet, or anything else you're holding in your right hand, so you won't screen yourself off with your arm or an object. Your unconscious mind takes care of all this for you. In fact, it could even be that you haven't yet noticed that this person is there. You've initiated a process of communication, whether you know it or not.

Your next step will be to begin observing him or her discreetly, with a sideward glance now and then, just enough to show your interest. In purely mechanical terms, you look at this person until he or she looks back. Then you maintain eye contact for a moment or two, before looking away again. You don't move your head, which is still facing the people you're there with. The only part of you that moves is your eyes. Women have access to a devastating weapon here. Women often, when they first start to look away again after having made eye contact, *look down at the ground* for a brief moment. This is what the expression "furtive glance" really refers to.

FLIRTING EXERCISE

If you're a woman, try this simple test. Imagine there is an attractive person at the other end of the room. Look at this person out of the corner of your eye, and then look away by moving your eyes to the other side. Look at the person again. But this time, when you look away, do it by looking down at the ground first. Did you notice any difference? Did it feel familiar somehow? I thought it might.

Looking down is an invitation. It's a sign of submission and says "I'm harmless" or even "I can/want to be conquered." I am well aware of how reactionary a statement like that might seem in our contemporary, #MeToo world. But unfortunately for our rational, enlightened minds, our unconscious flirtations often stem from a very primal programming from before we were human beings, and a lot of the time it revolves around the female's submission to the male. It may not be particularly politically correct or even tasteful when it comes to gender equality, but it's how these things work. It's been this way since the dawn of time, and we're far from the only creatures that behave this way. Most of the animal kingdom's mating rituals involve elements of female submission, and the human mating dance is no exception to this rule. Otherwise, men might simply never have the courage to approach women at all.

Showing Off Your Plumage

Now, let's go back to that room you were in. When you have (unconsciously) confirmed that the other person is watching you, you show off your beautiful plumage like a peacock. Or, rather, you do the human equivalent: you start trying to improve your looks for him or her. You adjust your clothing, hair, and jewelry. Your posture will become more alert and your back will straighten out. If you're a man, you will, at least in theory, show off your muscular chest to show what an alpha male you are. And if you're a woman you will present your assets in the best way you know how. To put it briefly: no matter who you are, you will start showing what you've got.

And if you're a woman, messing around with your hair or your earrings is a combined dual display. Just like other animals do to display submission, you expose your most sensitive body parts: your wrists. You also display your palms, which demonstrates that you aren't holding any rocks or other implements that you could use to knock the head in of any man who approaches you. Showing an empty hand is a very old and primitive way of displaying friendly intentions. Chimpanzees that are fighting do the same thing to show that they don't want to fight anymore. Even though we are no longer apes, our unconscious mind still registers the importance of the gesture, and we humans have even developed our own variants of it; the original reason why you extend your hand in greeting is actually to show that you are not holding a sword.

The Challenge

Now, it's time for the actual checkout. You show your interest by examining the person, which is done by squinting a little, tilting your head. You're checking him or her out. This is pretty much all we men have in our arsenals. If nothing has happened yet, we have to make a conscious decision to approach the person we've been unconsciously checking out.

Women still have another weapon at their disposal. It is as devastatingly simple as it is devastatingly deadly. Again, if you're a woman and can try this out while you're reading this, do it. You'll know exactly what I'm talking about. Here's the position: head and eyes go into checkout position as mentioned. Squint, and slant your head. Then place one hand on your hip, which you raise a little.

That's it. Now, as a woman, you're no longer being submissive, you're posing a real challenge. What this pose says is "I'm curious about you, but I wonder if you've got the guts to walk over here?" It doesn't get any more direct than that.

Remember, these are still unconscious techniques you're using. So, without knowing that you've done anything to encourage it, suddenly that person is standing there, right in front of you, wanting to talk to you. And you have no clue how it happened. You are also quite likely to be asked if you know each other, since you seem so familiar to him or her. Do you know whom you remind that person of? Himself or herself, of course, because you've been standing there following the person's body language!

Your Position Signals Trust and Interest

If you're standing (or sitting) facing directly toward each other, this is a strong sign of attraction, since you're literally exposing your vulnerable sides to each other. Usually, we stand at a 45-degree angle to each other when we speak, because facing each other directly is simply too intimate. Any animal knows the sides are the better protected parts of our bodies, thanks to our rib cages. Also, by standing at an angle, the body presents a smaller "target area" to any threats. To face each other directly, you either have to trust each other greatly, probably because you know each other well, or else doing so is a sign of attraction. For the same reason, it can be threatening if somebody approaches you from straight ahead. If you stand too close or tower over somebody, you will be perceived as intrusive and aggressive rather than humble and vulnerable.

If you turn straight toward somebody who isn't comfortable with it, the discomfort will often be expressed by that person touching his neck, collar, or necklace. It's a sign telling you to either back off physically or change the subject of conversation. You're either standing too close or talking about something that makes him uncomfortable.

Now that you're standing there, facing each other and talking, the technique of flirting takes on more nuance. You can use this opportunity to pay attention to the other person's unconscious behavior. Are the pupils dilated and signaling interest? Has his or her body language opened up, so there aren't any hands or anything else getting in the way between you? Also, make sure he or she is well rooted to the floor with both feet, and not about to head off somewhere. Now is the time to use the methods for rapport that you couldn't use when you were still some distance apart. If you do it the right way, you'll soon be taking turns following and leading each other's body language.

Let's imagine that your conversation has continued, and a little later, you've moved to a couch, or a chair each in the worst case. The same thing still goes. You keep dismantling any barriers between the two of you. Sitting cross-legged is a bad idea, even though it's a grounded position. The reason for this is that the leg also becomes a barrier. So both feet should be planted on the floor. Another barrier that is often removed at this point is glasses, which are either removed or pushed up to the forehead.

As you know, an interested person is alert, energetic, and often leans forward a little when you speak to him or her. Signs that somebody is uninterested, restless, or nervous can be gestural slips, which you read about earlier. If he or she is enjoying your company, hands and feet should be still and relaxed, not fidgeting or tapping on the floor. Pay attention to hands being moved to the face. Remember what you read in chapter 7 on lying.

Sensual Stuff

A new sign that will start appearing now, if it hasn't already, is discreet touching of oneself or an object, like a wineglass. Depending on how your relationship has developed, this could be a sign that he or she is feeling a little cornered, and needs to confirm his or her sense of reality. In those cases, the person will probably touch his or her neck, and his or her eyes will roam. But if the relationship is still good, these are no less than unconscious, symbolic caresses meant for you. A related behavior is putting things in your mouth, and I don't mean potato chips or cheese sandwiches. Now we start sucking on and chewing on olives, ice cubes, chocolate, or anything else that can be moved between our lips in a reasonably sensual way. We will often also start licking them (our lips, not the olives) a little. It might all sound a bit silly, but this is no joke. Who told you our unconscious minds are all sophisticated and stuff? There wouldn't really be any need for it, since we don't notice these things anyway. Watching somebody we're attracted to eating or drinking is almost an unbearable turn-on for our unconscious minds.

And as if that weren't enough, we decide to loosen up a little at this stage. Men will loosen their ties and unbutton their shirts, or remove their jacket or sweater, and women will let their hair out or at least start swinging one of their sandals off of their toes. What we're actually doing is beginning to get undressed. We aren't aware of anything besides having a very nice time at the moment, but the mating dance has just begun in earnest.

A True Story

I fully understand if you're having a hard time accepting that the behavior I am discussing is still unconscious. Surely you'd never miss such blatant attempts at seduction? Maybe you wouldn't if you were silently observing the person in question. But remember, you're busy thinking about the things you're talking about, listening to the other person, adding your own clever comments, and showing off your best behavior. There simply isn't time for you to think about these things consciously, especially when you're not quite sure what they mean.

Let me tell you a story that illustrates how unaware we really are.

A year or so ago, I was lecturing in a luxurious holiday resort in the Caribbean. As the weather was very hot, clothing was casual, sometimes minimal, even in the more-formal contexts. One night, we were at an outdoor restaurant, having dinner. A man who has become famous thanks to his impressive physique and size walked in and sat down. His presence was impossible to ignore, which was obvious, as all the guests gave him a quick look before returning to their meals.

A minute or so after he sat down, a young woman walked up to him. She had long, bleached hair, was about twenty-five, and was wearing a tank top with a lot of cleavage, a short skirt, and sandals. I was sitting too far away to hear their conversation, but I was able to study their behavior. He turned his chair away from the table to be able to face her directly, which I felt was a nice gesture, telling her he was prepared to give her his time and attention. (Of course, his size made it impossible for him to expose weakness or vulnerability to her in this way, but more important, he posed no threat either, as he was sitting down while she was standing up.) They spoke for two or three minutes.

During their conversation, here's what she did: first, she placed one hand on the table she was standing next to. Since the table was quite low, this means she was leaning to the side, supported by her arm, which made the arm a useful support for pushing her chest up and out toward him. Twenty seconds later, she moved her hand on the table forward a little more, making it necessary for her to lean forward slightly, which positioned her cleavage directly in line with the seated man's face. After another twenty seconds, she began touching her neck, but not in the nervous way. This was the sensual way: she casually dragged her finger in a caress along her necklace and the collar of her tank top. Half a minute went by like this, before her right sandal was removed, and she started rubbing her naked foot along her left leg. Up . . . and down. Up . . . and down.

I almost choked on my salad. How was he going to respond to this? Well, he did the exact opposite of what she was doing. He looked everywhere but at her, gave brief answers to her questions (I could see this even though I couldn't hear their words), tapped his feet on the floor, and kept moving his hands around. After a while, she had to give up, and she went back to her own table.

When their conversation had ended, I couldn't resist. I sought the woman out as soon as I could, and asked her what they had spoken about. She had perceived their conversation as strictly business related. As it happened, he had purchased a product from her about a year earlier, and she wanted to know if he was happy with it. She was deeply shocked when I described her behavior and the obvious attraction she had been displaying. She claimed that she had no memory at all of doing all the things I mentioned, and was quite concerned that she might have made an unprofessional impression. I believed her.

I also had a quick talk with the man. I began by saying that I understood that this must happen to him all the time and that it must be bothersome for him. He responded by admitting that this was true, but he told me he made an effort to give everybody the time they needed and to be nice and polite to everybody. When I described the behavior he had just displayed, he was as upset as the woman had been just before. He was worried he might have made a disrespectful or unsympathetic impression, and asked me if I thought he should apologize to her. I told him he probably didn't need to, since neither one of them had been aware of their own behavior, let alone the other's.

They were both textbook examples of everything you've been reading about here, and they really had no clue about it. At least not consciously. If I had asked their unconscious minds, I would almost certainly have had completely different answers. But they were both consciously convinced that what happened was that they had a brief, business-related conversation. Keep that in mind if you feel nervous about following somebody's body language; you can get away with a lot more than you might think.

When Interest Wanes

Back to you and the couch (or chairs). If, by this point, you've grown tired of the other person and have had enough, I'm sure you can guess which changes that boredom will cause in your behavior. You simply start making bad rapport. Barriers are re-erected: eyeglasses go back on, arms will start crossing the body (for instance, by holding things in your hands), legs are crossed under the chair, making the feet come off the ground, or are crossed at the thighs. The body tenses up. Eye contact is broken. Something a lot of people do is to suddenly seem more interested in flicking invisible dust away, or rubbing imaginary stains out of their clothes. Pretty soon the other person will get up and tell you she has just seen somebody she needs to talk to, excuse herself, and leave. When you return to your friends, and they ask you where you've been, you tell them you've spoken to somebody you didn't know for a while. That's it. The fact that you've just been dancing *sexy yes—sexy no* for half an hour is nowhere in your memory.

Everything I've been describing happens without a word. As you can guess, it's far from impossible to display this behavior, without even being particularly subtle about it, while having a completely commonplace conversation at the superficial level. But just think how effective it could be if your words matched your actions, too! You can make yourself dangerously irresistible by practicing your rapport and wordless communication.

In the earlier example, I have described a set of behaviors that can all be displayed, one after the other, in a single encounter, but of course this could go on for longer, or even just include a single sign or so each time. Like with two coworkers at the office: everybody just *knows* there's something going on, no matter how they deny it themselves, despite their every meeting at the copying machine being a cornucopia of exposed wrists, moistening of lips (*moistening*, not *licking*), and facing each other directly. This can go on forever, and if nothing else happens, it's very likely that it will.

Human beings are social animals. We require acknowledgment from others and to be permitted to acknowledge other members of our pack, to be able to feel good. It doesn't have to be more than that, unless you want it to, of course.

Up until this point, everything in this book has been about learning to observe the unconscious signs other people display, and learning about your own signs. You've been able to use this knowledge in various ways, but the basic premise has always been the same. Now we're ready for a new approach. In the next two chapters, you will learn techniques for real influence. The influence you can achieve by leading somebody into rapport, for example, is of a rather passive kind. In the next chapter, we're going to touch on actively influencing the opinions, ideas, and emotions of others—all things a good mind reader needs to be able to do.

Many of these techniques, like "hidden commands" from chapter 9, or "anchors" from chapter 10, can be used to improve other people's situations. Some of the other techniques are included to help you protect yourself, as you are under a constant barrage of sophisticated tricks that people play on you to get at your thoughts, usually for commercial or political ends.

9

Look Deep into My Eyes . . .

METHODS OF SUGGESTION AND
UNDETECTABLE INFLUENCE

*In which you learn about how your thoughts are
affected directly by others, and you make a deal with Spider-Man.*

*To make people feel or act in a certain way is not to manipulate
them.* —ALVIN A. ACHENBAUM, MARKETING EXPERT

The quote here comes from something Achenbaum said in a hearing with the US Federal Trade Commission, sometime in the 1970s. The Trade Commission was becoming a little concerned about the market forces' ability to influence people. Either Alvin was a very foolish man, or, and more likely, he was using vacuous speech in the way you read about in chapter 7 on lying. Of course, making people feel or act in a certain way is "to manipulate" them.

What Achenbaum is objecting to is the negative value we tend to attach to the word "manipulation." All it's actually about is being able to influence somebody else enough to cause change in the person's behavior, and the value of the change ought to determine the value of the action. Change for the better is positive, and change for the worse is negative.

I suspect Achenbaum unconsciously valued the term in a negative way and was in fact referring to the negative value, not the actual term per se. And in the end, it's actually up to you whether manipulation, or influence, is going to be a good thing or a bad thing. You've already gained a great insight into how we constantly influence and manipulate each other through our behavior. Sometimes we don't need more than a friendly "Hello!" and a smile to influence somebody else to give us a friendly greeting in return. Other times, it's a lot more complicated. I think you've also started to realize that since we do this all the time, whether we want to or not, there's only one way to make sure you're not influencing or manipulating somebody in a bad way. You need to know what it is you're doing so you can decide when to *not* do it or choose to do it differently.

The techniques that you've learned so far have mainly allowed you to identify the emotional states of others, giving you clues to how they feel and what they're thinking. As you've seen, these techniques can also be used to influence the mental processes of others, causing a change of mood in somebody by influencing the person's body language, establishing good relationships in meetings, or making somebody like you. But considered as techniques of influence, they are quite passive, as I've mentioned. Now I want to teach you more-active techniques of influence. But I also want you to remember something: our goal is, still, to influence others in ways that help them achieve insight and emotional states they may have had a hard time reaching on their own. We're always looking to help people achieve their absolute best and most useful state of mind. And that is all we should be looking to do, because influence is a double-edged sword. All of the techniques I am teaching you now, to enable you to help people, can also be used to destroy people completely. And this is an absolute no-no. If I find out you're using these things in the wrong way, I'll come after you with a big stick. I'm serious. As Spider-Man's Uncle Ben put it:

With great power comes great responsibility.

Subtle Proposals

Suggestions to Our Unconscious Minds

To use *suggestion* means to plant opinions, images, and thoughts in other people's minds without them being conscious of it. They believe that the new idea comes from them, whereas in fact they've had their perception of reality manipulated by someone else. The media in general, and advertisers in particular, use this technique a great deal. The editors of a large daily newspaper were well aware of these methods when they used the slogan "Who formed your opinions?" in their advertising for several years.

You could say that *a suggestion is a proposal to our unconscious.* Usually, proposals are made to our conscious minds, and we reflect upon and make up our minds about them once we have heard them. Often this is a question of behaving in a particular way or agreeing with some opinion or other. The reason why it's so much more efficient to propose things directly to our unconscious minds instead is that our unconscious minds don't analyze what's being said in the same way our conscious minds do.

If someone makes a proposal to our conscious minds, we filter the information; we analyze the content of the proposal and then make up our minds about it. Either we agree with the proposal: "I definitely want to go and eat with her"; or we reject it: "No, I'm not hungry"; or we request more information before deciding: "It depends on whether it's going to be sausages again." But a *suggestion* to our *unconscious mind* bypasses our conscious, analytical filters. As a result, we don't need to decide what we think about what's being said. Our unconscious mind interprets it all as objective truth. If someone says to us, "Oranges are tasty," we can consciously decide whether we agree or not. But if the same thing is provided as a suggestion to our unconscious mind, we will accept it as fact. As true. Oranges *are* tasty.

As well as having the media and advertisers bombard us with suggestions, we also use suggestions in our daily communication with one another. We are constantly making suggestions with our body language, as we saw in chapter 8 on flirting. But suggestions hidden within our language can also be extremely effective, and we're going to take a closer look at them now. Because, after all, it's much easier to read someone's mind if you've already decided what the person is going to be thinking about.

 Our unconscious mind doesn't filter and doesn't make judgments. It accepts propositions uncritically, as long as whatever is said doesn't clash too badly with the recipient's self-image or perception of reality.

Don't Think Like That

Negations, "Not," and Denials

A very common method for planting new ideas in someone is to claim that something *isn't* the case. Before we can "not do" something, we have to be able to imagine what it is that we are going to put after the word "not."

Don't think of a blue polar bear.

In order to understand that sentence, you have to be sure that you understand what a blue polar bear means, in order to apply the abstract concept of "not." And by then it's already too late. You've already thought of a blue polar bear.

If you see a newspaper headline that says "Ryan Reynolds denies romantic involvement with Emma Stone," you can't understand it without first understanding the concept "Emma Stone— romantic involvement—Ryan Reynolds," and then afterward adding the fact that this *isn't* the case. Even though this headline hasn't taught you anything new about the world, your mind still contains a new thought that wasn't there before. And as anyone who has, or has had, small children will know, the word "not" pales into insignificance pretty quickly compared to the rest of what's being said: Ryan Reynolds? Who would have guessed . . . ?

Negations Are Abstractions

This has to do with the fact that abstract concepts like "not" are the last things we learn when we are small. Because they are abstract and have no counterparts in the real world—unlike polar bears and Ryan Reynolds (although I'm not entirely sure about Reynolds)—they are difficult to remember. If you tell your child *not* to lean back on his chair, you're simultaneously planting the idea of leaning back on the chair. It's easy to conjure up an image of leaning back on a chair. The word "not" is a purely intellectual concept, which we have to remember to apply to the image, and that's difficult. Every time you tell your child not to lean back on the chair, you strengthen the image of leaning back on it. Eventually, it will be enough for the child to see the actual chair in order for the thought of leaning back on it to awaken in him—in spite of the fact that all you did was to ask him *not* to. Here are some more examples of how you can confuse people completely:

"I don't want to make you **lose count."**

"You're *not* **drinking** *anymore, are you?"*

"Stop **hitting your little brother!"**

Organizational consultant Jerry Richardson suggests a triple whammy:

"Don't **worry;** *it's* **not** *hard to find.* **You** *can't* **miss it!"**

Do you see what images or thoughts these sentences are planting in people's minds? It's true of all suggestions that the more someone is exposed to them, the stronger they will be. If you have had a drinking problem, and someone asks you once if you're still not drinking, there won't usually be a problem. But if the question is asked enough times, as formulated earlier, it will strengthen the mental image of *drinking* until your problem could easily be reawakened.

This is also the reason why children, when they are learning to ride a bike and how not to ride into things, behave like guided missiles. They are concentrating so hard on not *riding into the old lady,* not *riding into the old lady,* not *riding into the old lady,* that it becomes the only course of action open to them. Or, as I once did myself, driving a snow scooter into the only tree trunk within miles. A tree trunk that was six whole yards away from the scooter trail. The tree trunk that I was so very consciously trying not to *drive into.*

All kinds of people, from professional golfers to successful entrepreneurs, can tell you that if you concentrate on avoiding obstacles instead of concentrating on your goals, then you'll run straight into the obstacles. Now you know why. Don't think of a blue polar bear.

A Bad Word

I actually think that the word "not" ought to be banished from our language, because it is impossible to *not* do something. You are always doing *something*. Try telling a child not to do what he is doing. Compare that to telling the child what you want him to do instead, and notice the difference it makes. Adults function in precisely the same way. An action, like a thought, is energy in motion. It's impossible to stop energy once it's in motion. The only thing you can do is change it into something else. It's practically impossible to stop what you're doing and *not* do something or *not* think something. All you can do is divert the energy and think about *something else* instead.

So instead of asking somebody not to do something, and thereby planting an unnecessary thought that he may never have had otherwise (like the image of leaning back on a chair), tell him what you want him to do instead. The chance of getting what you want will be much higher. It will also force you to express yourself more creatively and positively than you would otherwise have done. But it's tricky!

Generally speaking, we need to get better at talking about things—and ourselves!—in terms of what those things are and what they can become, instead of talking about what things *aren't* and what they *can't be*. Things are what we say they are. Depending on what we say they are, we create different images, different suggestions, within ourselves—and within those around us. Remember Nixon's "I am not a crook"? You can be an alcoholic who doesn't drink. Or you can be sober. You can try to not be sad. Or you can try to be happy.

I recently spoke to someone who had been through a divorce six months earlier. He was still depressed. But much of his attitude to life changed when I got him to change his way of seeing things and to start thinking of himself as single rather than divorced. How you describe the world has an effect on the ideas you give yourself and those around you, which will in turn affect how you go through life. Are you moving forward? Or are you not moving backward? Which would you prefer?

"NOT" EXERCISE

Try to avoid using the word "not" for a whole day—and see how often you use it for convenience. It's a lot easier to tell somebody what you *don't* want than to explain what you *do* want. But if you make yourself do it, you'll find you will become a lot more expressive and positive every time you do *not* use "not."

Unwarranted Denial

A suggestion using "not" is the strongest when it is unexpected. By saying you yourself are or aren't doing something, you're also indirectly saying something about everybody else. If Nixon had intonated his famous line differently, and instead of saying, "I am *not* a crook," had said, "*I* am not a crook," that would have indirectly implied that there were others who *were* crooks.

Denouncing something, or suddenly offering a disclaimer, is a clever way to say things about other people. A politician who says, "*Our* party isn't xenophobic," is implicitly stating that some other parties are. Or is he? Actually, the politician said no such thing. But this is still the thought that appears in our heads. Because if it's not *their* party that's xenophobic, it must be that other one that is, right? And now I've made up my mind about how to vote in the next election. Until I read a new headline, that is, and forget all about it. But of course, I try . . . *not* . . . to forget it.

Take Charge

Speaking on Several Different Levels

There are other ways of hiding suggestions and proposals to the unconscious, too. When we talk to each other, what we really mean isn't always too clear. It can be interpreted in different ways. If all we did was listen to the words, we'd often have misunderstandings. But by also paying attention to tone of voice, body language, and the context, we can get a better understanding of what somebody's trying to tell us. We decide on a reasonable interpretation of what we're hearing, and then answer people based on that.

But our unconscious mind registers all of the different possible interpretations of the words. This means that it's possible to speak on several different levels at once. The interpretation of what we're hearing, which we are provided with by our conscious minds (and which we believe to be the correct interpretation), is the top level. Beneath it, we can express ourselves in ways so that what we say is open to another interpretation. This interpretation will be picked up by our unconscious. And if this "hidden" message is constantly expressed, our unconscious mind will begin to react to it.

I realize this sounds complicated, but bear with me, and you'll get it all in a moment. A simple example would be if somebody told me, "I'm starting to feel ill, Henrik." My conscious interpretation is that the person is starting to feel ill and wants to let me know about it. But there is another, hidden meaning in the suggestion: "I'm starting to **feel ill, Henrik**." This is called an embedded command. Now, a single one of these isn't very effective in isolation. But if the person who says it uses enough of these hidden suggestions, I will begin to react to them and start to feel ill—without any idea why.

"I'm starting to feel ill, Henrik. I feel like I have an upset stomach and want to throw up. You know the feeling. . . . "

I wouldn't recommend reading the last few lines too many times!

If you want to use suggestions in this way, you can strengthen their impact by emphasizing them carefully. Change your tone of voice or seek eye contact when you speak the words that are part of your suggestion. Do it exactly the same way for each suggestion. All you need for the unconscious mind of the person you're trying to influence to get the idea is to treat the things you say with a slightly lower voice as though they're special. The earlier examples of negations, using "not," also contain these hidden commands ("lose count," "you're . . . drinking") that you can emphasize using your tone of voice.

If you're starting to think this all seems like some kind of hypnosis, you're not far off the mark. This isn't hypnosis, but hypnosis exploits the way we understand speech. Hidden commands are part of hypnotic speech. In hypnotherapy, as in many other forms of therapy, the fact that we have several levels of understanding is used to great advantage. Using suggestion, you can give therapeutic suggestions to the client's unconscious, without being noticed. The father of modern hypnosis, Milton H. Erickson, whom I have mentioned several times, was unrivaled when it came to communicating on two levels at the same time like this.

Unintended Suggestions

You should always be on the lookout for hidden suggestions from other people, whether they are presented as regular proposals or as statements including the word "not." Lots of people use negative suggestions all the time without being aware of it. In this way, they unknowingly cause a lot of anxiety. Avoid these kinds of people whenever possible. Even if you should discover the suggestions, it may be difficult to avoid being influenced by them. You could also try responding with a rephrasing of what was just said, but with a positive suggestion instead.

If somebody is spreading bad vibes around, in the worst case, you can always use opinion aikido to establish rapport first: "I understand exactly how you feel. I would feel the same way if I were you."

Then, once you can tell that the person is listening to you, you give him or her positive suggestions, which are subtly emphasized with tone of voice and eye contact, in combination with an actual proposal for creative action: "I've noticed that I **feel much better**, since I said to myself, '**Hey you! Take a vacation.**'" Turn people's own weapons against them.

Any Word Can Be a Suggestion

Any word or expression is a potential suggestion, since our unconscious mind scans all possible interpretations and makes all available associations from all of the different messages we are exposed to every day. The next time you listen to a radio commercial or watch a commercial on TV, try listening to the different words and phrases used in it. If the commercial is any good, every word will have been carefully selected, with a certain effect that it is intended to have on you. Hidden suggestions can awaken associations you weren't expecting at all. If you use them in the right way, you can connect almost any associations you like to pretty much any product.

Today, the act of eating ice cream as a symbol for sex is a cliché of advertising. But, apart from in the purely Freudian sense, the relationship between ice cream and sex was a chance creation. Somebody at an ad agency had to have decided to connect ice cream to sexual suggestions, probably urged on by some motivation analyst like Ernest Dichter or Louis Cheskin, who had figured out that it ought to work. It worked so well that everybody else has been doing it ever since. But it could just as well have been about something completely different.

In advertisements, both on TV and on radio, specific words are used to put you in a specific mental or emotional state. This state is then associated with the product or the company's logo. Words like "warm," "soft," "clean," "powerful," and "bigger" put you in a completely different state and experience than words like "tense," "worried," "afraid," and "weak." The best way to make somebody feel something, then, is to talk about it. I don't know about you, but right now I have a bit of an itch in my throat. How about your throat? Isn't it a little itchy, too, when you think about it?

I thought it might be.

Or how about the ad I saw at a newsstand in an airport, which read "Do you remember how thirsty you get on an airplane?" Coincidentally, this offer was given at the same time as the new security measures for flights were applied, the ones that mean you can't bring a bottle of water onto the plane—unless you buy it after the security checkpoint. More precisely, at this newsstand.

Any word, expression, emotion, or image that you use when you're speaking to somebody will lead her into specific emotional states and experiences, in the same way that your wordless communication does. So make sure the place where you're leading her is where you want her to go, and not somewhere else.

ATTENTION EXERCISE

1. Find ten ordinary sentences that contain hidden suggestions, like "*not* statements," repetition-of-value terms, or hidden commands. Think about the things you hear yourself and others say.

2. Choose a newspaper, and try to find hidden suggestions, like *not* statements, repeated value terms, or hidden commands. Begin by looking at one of the editorials. Then see how many you can find in an article that is supposed to be reporting the news objectively.

I'm Not the One Who Said It

Suggestion Through Implication

An effective way of using linguistic suggestions is to hide them *between* the words, as insinuations or implications, rather than stating them directly. As you'll see, this works very well, and we usually don't have any idea what's going on when we hear these things, either.

Leaving Information Out

When we talk to each other, we often take a lot of linguistic shortcuts. We assume the person we're speaking to has the same understanding and definitions we have, and that the words mean the same to both of us. Therefore, we don't need to explain what we mean by every single word we use. This is a good thing, because talking the long way would be very bothersome. We routinely leave out a whole load of information that we take for granted when we talk to each other. Often, this won't be a problem. "It was pitch-dark out" will tend to be understood in more or less the same way, since people's concepts of "pitch-dark" won't vary too much. Value statements are a lot more troublesome. "The Oscars gala dinner was quite nice." How nice is "quite nice" to you, as opposed to me?

Sometimes, we leave too much information out, or it turns out the person we're talking to understands certain things in a different way than we do. That's when misunderstandings happen. We can also consciously leave information out, on the notion that "you know what I'm talking about." Or: "And as usual, he gave me that look, you know." The truth is, I might not know at all. I might just think I know. Then we'd be thinking about two different things, both convinced the one we're thinking of is the real intended meaning.

Using Comparisons Without Reference

A good example of leaving information out is the wording on the packaging of frozen food in our supermarkets. I have some frozen salmon in my microwave right now. The box says, "Now, we use our own stock in the sauce, which makes it taste better and gives it more depth. . . ." A while back, it seemed like there was some rule for manufacturers that they had to write things like the following on their boxes and bottles:

New better recipe!
New sauce for better taste!
New improved formula!
Now even whiter!

I don't doubt that all of this is true. The question is just what the comparison is to be made with. Better than what? Whiter than what? Better tasting and more improved than what? All of these statements are comparisons, but they leave out the thing that the comparison is made to. Our minds like things to make sense and love to see connections between things, to the point that we will create them if they don't exist. When we read phrases like the ones I just mentioned, we unconsciously fill in the blanks ourselves. We're so used to doing it that we automatically believe we know what the comparison is made with, and fill in our own interpretation, convinced it is the only right one.

"New sauce with more flavor!" They must mean more flavor than before, right? But the truth is there is a multitude of different, just-as-plausible interpretations: more flavor—than our other products; more flavor—than our competitors' products; more flavor—than before, but still pretty bland; and so on. Some interpretations will seem more plausible than others: "more flavor than cucumber" may seem like a less-plausible interpretation to some, but how do we know that's not the intended meaning?

Different people will make different interpretations. The only thing they will have in common is that they will all choose an interpretation they believe in and that they believe to be the only plausible interpretation. We will also prefer the interpretation that has the most personal relevance to us, as it will be the first one we'll think of. By consciously leaving information out in this way, you can make the recipients of the message fill it in with meaning themselves. In other words, by not really saying anything, you can make someone experience something that is both true and personally relevant to that person. This is a very clever way of establishing a personal relationship to the reader. You also make it the recipient's job to come up with good stuff that's true about the product. You don't even need to say anything!

By leaving information out, or by expressing yourself in ambiguous ways, you can make the recipient fill in the content, which guarantees that he or she will find it both true and personal. A copywriter I spoke to told me he loved using this particular gambit to get the reader emotionally involved.

We Think They Know

By speaking of somebody in general terms, so that the person has to fill in the blanks herself, you can also give an impression of knowing more about him or her than you actually do. A good example of this is the "interrogation method," which was used in China during the 1950s. When somebody was arrested, she was basically told only that "We know it all; you may as well confess." Then the poor prisoner was simply left in her cell for a few days to try to figure out what they actually meant. At last, after enough thinking, everybody always came up with something they'd done that they felt had to be the crime they were suspected of. The problem was that each confession was met with the statement that even if what she had confessed to was a serious crime, it wasn't the crime she was suspected of. Back to the cell, or back to some more creative interrogation methods, until the poor victim had confessed every act in her entire life as a potential crime toward the government.

This method can also be used to win people's trust. Express yourself about something in personal terms, but be ambiguous enough that the listener has to fill in all of the blanks herself.

While you're reading this, make a tight fist with one of your hands. Done it yet? Good. Keep it like that for a few seconds.

A few more.

Now, begin to open your hand, very slowly. Right about *now* you should have a rather odd sensation in your hand, right?

Good.

To be completely honest, I have no idea how your hand felt. It might have felt tingly, or itchy, or sweaty, or you may have felt that your hand was unusually warm. Or it could have been something else entirely. I left out enough information and expressed myself with enough ambiguity ("a rather odd sensation in your hand") to make you fill in all the blanks of what I actually meant by it. And you did, by assuming that what I was referring to was whatever specific sensation you had in your hand. A sensation that I didn't actually have any knowledge of. This way, you can make it seem like you know everything about somebody, even his most intimate secrets, by making him define for himself the things you're talking about. This technique is used by religious leaders, in police interrogations, and by unscrupulous confidence tricksters.

Public Outrages and Other Generalizations

Another way of using suggestion by implication is by using generalizations. A generalization is a statement that claims that everything in a certain category shares a certain trait. If you say that all Scots are misers, you've made a broad generalization about everybody who lives in Scotland. Words that are commonly used in generalizations include "all," "none," "always," "all the time," "never," "everywhere," and so on. (Note that even seemingly specific words like "immigrants" or "kids" are actually broad generalizations.) By using these words, you erase any obvious or subtle differences that are actually there, and give a very simplified account of things.

We often use generalizations in our speech in everyday situations. There is also a certain type of generalization that you come across in the news, like in our Swedish evening papers, which are full of phrases like "in the face of growing criticism," "in a telephone poll," or, my personal favorite, "public outrage." But what do they really mean? How much does criticism need to be growing for it to be acceptable to claim that it is growing? Because honestly, for it to be true, strictly speaking, no more would actually be required than for an angry email to show up on Monday, and then another one on Tuesday. How many people do you need to call to make it a telephone poll? Two hundred? Twenty? Two?

You might think I'm exaggerating, but I'm not. A journalist once told me that his newspaper demanded that there be three or four upset people in order to use the phrase "public outrage" in an article. I can't vouch for the truth of this, but it doesn't sound too far-fetched. Especially when you consider that when propaganda expert Martin Borgs worked at a newspaper, its definition of an "outrage" meant ten angry letters from its readers.

So what's the problem with this, then? Well, by using these kinds of words, we make it sound as though there is a consensus out there, when this could actually be untrue. We don't react consciously to these words; in fact we almost don't even hear them. But they still leave us with a feeling that this is something people seem to have a certain opinion about. Maybe even most people, seeing as it's an "outrage" and everything. In this way, you can *create* a public opinion out of nothing. We don't want people to think we're stupid, so to play it safe, we tend to think the same as everybody else does. And if it's true, as the paper says, that something is facing "growing criticism," maybe I should consider taking a stand against that thing the people seem so upset about, right? This is a good way of influencing public opinion and making people think what you want them to, by using generalizations that imply that most people are already feeling this way, when there's actually only a handful—perhaps no more than ten—people involved.

Watch Out for Abstractions

The last method for hiding suggestions in implications is a variation of the vacuous rhetoric I mentioned in the section on lying. By expressing yourself in an extremely specific way, but simultaneously avoiding defining the words and terms you use, you can make it sound like you're supporting or even proving a claim, without actually having provided any real information at all. An example of this is the business manager under pressure who said, "The first thing we need to do is discuss this new, difficult situation we're in, as it affects important elements in our continuous process of growth." Sounds good enough, I guess. But he never told everybody what that situation was, or why it was so difficult, and I doubt anybody really felt particularly illuminated. Besides, what are those supposedly important elements he was talking about? What process, and how long has it been going on for, anyway?

Journalists are familiar with this trick of using excessive abstraction, and if they're any good, they have very little patience for this kind of thing. Media coaches will often warn their clients that they can only get away with three consecutive uses of excessive abstraction before losing credibility. The hard part is to discover it at all as a listener. It sounds good, often very good, even. But in writing, it will often look absurd.

You're One Big Suggestion

In fact, it's not just your words that suggest things to others. Your entire presence, what you're wearing, how you move, and how you sound are all important, too. The whole idea of leading somebody into rapport can be considered a giving of suggestions that the other person follows. Martin Borgs, in his book *Propaganda*, gives an example of how he used his own body for suggestion to influence a decision when he wanted to be discharged from the hospital a day early. The problem was that this was a Sunday, when nobody is usually discharged:

> *The first step was to ask the nurse to tell the doctor I wanted to see him. Before the doctor arrived, I freshened myself up. Took off the huge hospital shirt. Took a shower. Put some jeans and a sweater on. Tidied the room, and put everything in its right place. Packed my stuff in bags, and left them in a visible spot on the floor. Then, I sat down in the chair to type on my computer, instead of lying in bed watching TV.*

The unstated implication couldn't have been clearer. The doctor wasn't meeting a sick, weak man, but a healthy man with good, strong energy levels. Martin was discharged the very same day.

Think about your body language, the way you speak, your clothes, and the way you act. What suggestions are you giving people about yourself? And what suggestions would you *like* to be giving them?

The methods of influence this chapter has touched on have mainly been methods for influencing the *opinions* of others, but people's emotions can be influenced, too. The next chapter will teach you how to use *anchors,* which allow you to activate the desired emotions in yourself and in others, with speed and great precision. Remember the things you've already learned about how our actions are controlled by our emotions, and you'll realize the power this kind of influence has. But remember, you have to give up all your ambitions of world domination and planting Manchurian candidates before I'll allow you to read on.

10

Haul Anchors

HOW TO PLANT AND TRIGGER
EMOTIONAL STATES

*In which you will get in touch with your own
feelings and those of others, dodge a hug, and
lose your fear of sharks.*

As you know, you can influence the emotional states of others by means of rapport and suggestion. However, the results will often be a little imprecise (e.g., how do you lead someone toward "excited and confident" as opposed to "happy and creative"?), and you might have a hard time achieving strong emotional reactions. There is a more effective way of influencing emotions, which allows you to trigger any emotion you like in anybody you like whenever you like, and this more effective way is the use of anchors.

Anchors = imprints

There's actually no real difference between an anchor and an imprint, which is what Pavlov was making when he got his dogs to produce saliva when he rang a bell. The difference is that we're imprinting people, not dogs, and the things we're imprinting are emotional states, not drooling. This means that you can quickly turn other people's negative emotional states into positive ones using anchors. Since any emotion can be anchored, you will be able to produce emotions like an inclination to buy something, to worship, or to exhibit nervous tension.

So don't forget what Spider-Man's Uncle Ben told you. Use your new knowledge responsibly, and only use your powers for good. There are plenty of people who have tried going down the other path, and they'll tell you that whatever goes around comes around. And besides, if you exploit people in this life, you'll spend your next life as a rock. So be good. It's better to give the people you meet something special to remember than to help them get even more neurotic.

You're Already Full of Anchors

I've said it before, and I'll say it again: nothing in this book is really news to you. This is true of anchors as well. You use them all the time already. We have lots of experiences as we go through our lives. Many of these experiences will also be tied to strong emotional states like joy, love, hate, betrayal, happiness, nervous tension, anger, and so on. When we're reminded of something we've experienced, we remember more than just the event. To some extent, we also start to feel the same as we did at the time. We don't actually even need to remember the event; we can bring back the emotions from events we've even forgotten. That's why we can see somebody from afar and instinctively feel dislike for her. It's not until afterward that we realize she resembles somebody who used to bully us at school, or that she was wearing the same type of sweater our childhood enemy used to wear.

The thing that triggers one of these emotional reactions to a memory, in this case a certain look or item of clothing, is known as an *anchor*. It's a situation, object, or experience that we unconsciously associate with a certain emotion. Its appearance, like the sweater, plays some role in the specific memory with which the emotion is associated. Make sense? We come across anchors all the time, like when we hear a song we know and have the same emotions we did when we heard it the first time. "Hey, they're playing our song! Devo! Remember . . . ?" Or like going through albums full of old photos, awakening memories and the emotions that go with them. And let's not forget movie soundtracks! In many films, the music is used as an anchor, to get the audience into the right emotional state.

Two of the best examples of this are Fritz Lang's *M,* and Steven Spielberg's *Jaws*. In *M,* the killer whistled "In the Hall of the Mountain King" by Grieg every time he appeared. In the end, just hearing the whistling was enough to make the audience understand that the killer was approaching, without him having to appear on screen. This trick may have given people the shivers in 1931, but audiences are a little more sophisticated these days. Right? Forty-four years later, Spielberg used the famous theme from *Jaws* in exactly the same way Lang did, to indicate that the shark was approaching.

I know several people who saw *Jaws* when they were around the age of twelve, who still experience a significantly elevated pulse, sweating, anxiety, and nervous twitches every time I sneak up behind them to hum: *"Duhm-duhm . . . duhm-duhm-DUHM-DUHM-duhm-duhm-DUHM-DUHM!!!"* How's that for an anchor?

Places can make for strong anchors. A friend of mine figured this out on her own recently when she broke up with her boyfriend. The conversation between the two of them began in bed at her place, but when the tears and anger came out, she quickly realized they had to finish the conversation in the kitchen instead. As she explained it to me: "Otherwise all of those horrible, sad emotions would have stayed there in my bed. They would have come back every time I went to bed to go to sleep, and of course I didn't want that." Fortunately, she realized her bed was turning into a powerful negative anchor before it was too late. But as luck would have it, we're not always this perceptive.

The strongest anchors are often the sensory impressions that we give the least thought to: tastes and smells. One of the most famous examples of an anchor in human culture is the one described by author Marcel Proust in his novel *In Search of Lost Time,* wherein the main character eats a little cake he has just dunked in his cup of tea—and suddenly remembers his entire childhood:

And suddenly the memory returns. The taste was that of the little crumb of madeleine which on Sunday mornings at Combray . . . when I went to say good day to her in her bedroom, my aunt Léonie used to give me, dipping it first in her own cup of real or of lime-flower tea. . . . But when from a long-distant past nothing subsists, after the people are dead, after the things are broken and scattered, still, alone . . . the smell and taste of things remain. . . . And once I had recognized the taste of the crumb of madeleine soaked in her decoction of lime-flowers which my aunt used to give me . . . immediately the old grey house upon the street, where her room was, rose up like the scenery of a theatre . . . and the whole of Combray and of its surroundings, taking their proper shapes and growing solid, sprang into being, town and gardens alike, from my cup of tea.

Anchors on Cue

The anchors we are interested in here are not of the kind Proust was talking about. The kind we are dealing with are anchors that can provoke different emotional states in people. Of course, it would be very useful if we could know exactly which anchors lie hidden in the unconscious minds of ourselves and others, so we could simply trigger them at will. Feeling a little drained? Trigger your energy anchor, and *BOOM!!* Just like that, you've turned yourself into the Energizer Bunny. In this way, we could influence ourselves and others to always feel as happy as possible, and to always be in a creative, exciting state of mind. But since the anchors are hidden in the unconscious mind, it's very hard to know what they are. This might make it sound like it's time to give up, but that would be premature. You see, we can easily *create new* anchors, in ourselves as well as in others. And we're always doing it anyway, so we might as well learn to do it effectively. By creating new anchors, you will always know exactly which emotion is being triggered and exactly what to do to trigger it.

Here's how it works: whatever you do or say when you're with somebody who is experiencing a strong emotion will become linked to the emotion in the other person's memories. That particular action will be your anchor. At a later time, when you repeat it, saying or doing the same thing as before, this will stimulate the memory of the emotional state that person was in when the anchor was planted. How much of the emotion is reawakened, and whether the emotion is as powerful as before or just a pale shadow of a memory, depends on how well you managed to plant the anchor in the first place.

By making yourself aware of how anchors are made, you will also get a better sense of the anchors you plant in people unintentionally. The same goes for anchors you plant in yourself, like the one my friend almost planted in her bedroom. And, of course, you'll also have a better chance of noticing what anchors other people plant in you, intentionally or otherwise. Anchors, like suggestions, are often used in the wrong way.

Unconscious and Negative Anchors

Jerry Richardson, mentioned earlier, gives a good example, in which a father notices that his son is sad, and hugs him. The father's intention, of course, is to give comfort and support. The problem is that his hug has to have been used in a positive context before, that is, been anchored with positive emotions, for the positive emotions to be triggered when he hugs his sad little boy. But this father doesn't have a lot of physical contact with his children. In fact, it only really happens when he needs to comfort them. So instead of this hug being associated with something pleasant, and the father being able to use it to counteract the negatives, his hug will be anchored with the negative emotional state, since that's when the child experiences it.

If this happens a few times in a row, every time the father hugs his son, he will be putting him in a negative state, even if the son was happy to begin with. If physical touch is used only when somebody is sad, that emotion will be associated with the touch, whatever the intentions behind it are.

Unfortunately, we tend to touch people more when they are sad or upset. Richardson wonders if this might explain why so many people in our society don't like being touched; they've simply learned, since their childhood, to associate touch with negative emotions. This is a frightening thought. We need to become more aware of our behavior, since the memory of how somebody behaved will be stored in our unconscious mind, along with the memory of the emotion we experienced at the time.

Generally speaking, it's a good idea to make physical contact with somebody who's in a good mood. In this way, you can help him when he feels less happy, by touching him and triggering his current, positive emotions.

Of course, an emotional anchor doesn't have to involve any touching. I used touching in the example because physical contact is a common way of giving comfort and support, and because anchors using touch tend to be very strong. But as I wrote previously, anything we can perceive can make a functional anchor—a word, an image, a tone of voice, a particular gesture, a smell, a color, or a taste. Combining various sensory impressions in an anchor is even better. Instead of just saying a word, you do it with a specific tone of voice while making a gesture with one hand and touching her arm with the other hand. The more sensory impressions you can include in the anchor, the clearer and stronger it will be.

Altering Other People's Mental States

You know that the mood you're in, and whatever is going through your head at the moment, has a great effect on how you perceive the things you're told, and whether you'll find a particular idea wonderful or terrible. If you have an idea or a proposition you'd like somebody to listen to, and preferably agree to, you need her to be in as receptive an emotional state as possible. If she isn't, and you don't have the tools to alter her emotional state, you could end up in trouble. Establishing rapport is the most important tool for this. But even if you get her to like you and want to be open to your ideas, she might still be sad or upset about something you can't do anything about. It could be something that has nothing to do with your relationship to her, maybe something to do with her private affairs.

Even though her intentions are good, the emotions she's carrying around will still affect her attitude to your idea, even if the reason for her state has nothing to do with you. By using a positive anchor, you can alter her emotional state to make it more suitable for your meeting, at least temporarily.

You can also use an anchor to strengthen somebody's emotional response to a certain suggestion. Like the car salesman who asks his customer, "How do you feel about making a deal right away?" and then simultaneously triggers an anchor to make his customer experience strong feelings of joy.

Anchors work because of the way we associate things that happen inside our minds—how we feel or what we're thinking—to events in the world outside us. It doesn't matter if the two are directly connected or not. This is how anchors are created, but it's also one of the reasons why knowing how to use them is so important. If you meet somebody who is in a negative state, and you don't know how to get him out of it, you run the risk of having your entire meeting become an anchor for his negative emotional state! Then, every time he meets you or hears of you he will feel slightly uncomfortable or unhappy, and he won't understand why. That's not quite the feeling you want other people to have for you, is it? It can actually have a devastating effect, both on your private life and on your career. Fortunately, the opposite is true as well: if you're good at awakening positive, great emotions in other people, by using the skills you've learned from this book, you will make yourself into an anchor for these emotions. If the anchor is strong enough, all that will be required to trigger these positive emotions, or whatever the emotions you've planted are, is for somebody to mention you by name.

As I said earlier, you can plant anchors in yourself, too. This is a good way to give yourself a well-needed boost of any emotion you need. You could make yourself confident before a situation that would otherwise make you nervous, happy when you're down, or energetic and determined when you're feeling lazy, and so on.

You can also combine several different emotions into a single anchor. I have an anchor for myself that triggers a mixed emotion with elements of joy, pride, curiosity, some butterflies in the stomach, and a healthy dose of self-confidence. The effect is almost intoxicating. I trigger it every time I'm about to go onstage to perform one of my shows, and it gets me into the exact right frame of mind to allow me to give the performance my absolute best.

Now, I want to teach you how to make your own anchors. I suggest you don't just read this. Try it out for yourself at once. That's the only way to make yourself understand how simple it actually is and how well it works. It may sound like magic, but it's really no more mystical than the effect on Pavlov's pooches. The fact is, it's the exact same thing, just more fun and a lot quicker.

It's That Human Touch

How to Plant an Anchor

Exactly *what* you should do (gesture, word, touch, or something else) depends on what you'd like to use and what the situation allows for. As I wrote earlier, touch is a strong anchor for most people, but some situations don't allow for any touch beyond the initial handshake. Perhaps you're simply too far from the other person to be able to touch him or her in a natural way. In situations like this you should get good results if you use a clear, accentuated gesture and say something. The gesture should be something you don't normally do, like clapping your hands, a quick drumroll using your fingers, slapping your forehead, or a very distinctive facial expression.

What makes using a word so useful is that you can "hide" the word in your speech when you want to trigger the anchor. In fact, the word you use to trigger the anchor doesn't even have to be the same word that you used to plant the anchor, as long as it sounds very similar and you intonate it the same way. An example of how words can be used along with body language to make an anchor:

*To establish the anchor, you make a specific gesture or touch while saying (at the golf course, for example), "What a **great** swing!" Emphasize the word "**great**."*

*To trigger the anchor at a later time, such as in a meeting, you make the same gesture or touch, while saying, "I'm convinced this will be a **great** solution for you. How do you feel about it?" Intonate "**great**" the same way you did when you planted the anchor.*

An example of the use of similar words:

Planting the anchor: "**Good** *job!*"
Triggering the anchor: "*We* **should** *go!*"

In both cases, **good/should** are intonated the same way and spoken at the same moment as any gesture or touch you're using.

Do you remember the car salesman? What he does, by saying something like: "I'm sure this will be a **good** solution for you. How do you feel about it?" (or a more direct version: "Let's make a deal! **Good!**"), while tapping you lightly on your shoulder, is to make you feel something similar to the feeling you got when he planted the word "**good**" along with a tap to the shoulder. He did this while telling you an amusing anecdote, and you never noticed a thing. Now that you're back in that emotional state again, you have an easier time understanding all of the benefits of making a deal right away.

In the same way, you can use anchors yourself to associate positive emotions with your suggestions and ideas. Of course, these should be emotions your suggestion awakens in you, as well. You should never trigger emotional states that aren't justified in other people.

If you want to see examples of industries that have developed great expertise in this area, have a look at TV and newspaper advertising. Ads are also a good way to practice identifying anchors that we don't think about, but ones that affect most of us. You'll notice that the ads use more than just suggestion. They will also often exploit cultural and social triggers, like symbols, colors, and sounds, to awaken specific emotional states in you, in an attempt to associate the emotions you're feeling with the product the company sells. The anchor for the emotional state is the product itself. It might not sound too devious to make people feel happy when they see the Coca-Cola logo. But you can just as well imprint an inclination to buy that is triggered every time somebody sees the latest Nike sneakers.

Look at the advertisements. It's quite obvious there are some people out there who've never even heard of Spider-Man's uncle.

The Pavlovian Bells, the Pavlovian Bells!

Finding the Right Moment

The easiest way to plant an anchor in somebody is to wait until he or she is in the emotional state you're after. Let's say it's joy. When you notice something happening that makes him or her a lot happier than usual for a moment, like a good laugh at the movies or a hole in one on the golf course, you plant the anchor, just when you believe the emotion to be at its strongest. It's important that you try to plant the anchor as the emotion is growing, or peaking. You don't want an anchor that's associated with an ebbing emotion.

When using this method, the problem is that waiting for the person to have the emotion that you want to make an anchor for can be very time-consuming. Besides, you run the risk of acting a bit like a stalker. The person in question will start wondering about your constant presence, and there is a limit to how much you can follow somebody around before you get tagged with a restraining order. But using natural emotional states is still a great method for planting improvised anchors. Make a habit of always making an anchor when you notice that somebody is very happy. Why not, if the emotion is there anyway? Even if you hadn't planned it, you never know when it will come in handy later on.

So am I actually saying that you should be planting anchors in everybody you meet, the moment they have a strong, positive emotion? You bet I am. There's nothing to it. Once you've tried it a few times, you'll begin to do it automatically, with hardly any effort at all on your part.

But what if you don't feel like waiting for somebody to end up in the emotional state you want to anchor? Then you have to make sure to trigger that state in her *yourself*! As you recall from chapter 5, emotions can be triggered in a number of different ways. Anchoring just happens to be less detectable, and quicker, than most of the other methods. The other methods will often awaken emotions by using associations of thoughts. Anchors and imprints function more like physical reflexes. But if you want to anchor joy in somebody, why not tell a good joke? Plant your anchor while they're heaving with laughter. Or maybe you want to provoke a sense of "going for it"? Or belonging? Then start talking about it, and make her recall a time when she felt that particular emotion. Make sure you're using the right sensory words to establish strong associations as you lead her into her memory. Make sure she's having the emotion again. You might say something like:

> *"You know how you sometimes have an idea, that you just know you have to realize, or when you see something you just have to own at any cost? Know what I mean? When that feeling fills you completely, and you can't stop thinking that you simply must have this thing? Or do this thing? Do you remember the feeling?"*

Use your perception to determine when the emotion is at its strongest. It won't be hard to see, as you already know what the physical signs of involvement and interest are: clear eyes, dilated pupils, changes in the skin tone in the face as blood circulation increases, and so on. Plant the anchor at the moment when the emotion seems to be at its peak.

Don't worry about how to lead your conversation into having the other person relive an experience. It's a common way of talking to people, and we use it all the time: "Do you remember . . . ?" is a completely ordinary expression to use in any conversation. In everyday speech, we're constantly triggering emotional associations in each other. You can explain to the person that you want to make sure he or she knows that the feeling is the result of your desire to have him or her understand your own feelings concerning the issue at hand, whatever it may be.

> *". . . Do you remember the feeling? Can you feel it right now? That's the exact way I feel about this."*

You can also use phrases such as the following:

"What's your favorite thing about . . ."
"Can you remember the last time you felt . . ."
"Imagine that you . . ."

As the last phrase implies, you don't necessarily have to be awakening an actual memory in the person you're talking to. For, as you know, emotions can be awoken just as well by the imagination:

"Wouldn't it be great if . . . ? How would that make you feel?"

ANCHOR EXERCISE

To create an anchor in yourself (why wouldn't you?), you would go about it the same way as when you're creating one in somebody else: decide on an emotion and find a memory, or imagine an experience where this emotion is strong. Relive the memory, reawaken the emotion, and anchor it. Use the following looping method to make the anchor as strong as possible:

Step 1. Decide on the emotion you want to be able to trigger with an anchor. Find a memory or imagine a scenario in which that emotion is strong.

Step 2. Build up the memory or imagined scene, one sense at a time. First visualize the way things look, like buildings, people, colors, or lighting. The more detail the better. Then add any suitable sounds. Are there waves beating? Joyful cheering? Leaves rustling in the wind? Any animals making noise? Last, add any bodily sensation or scents, like wind, heat, sweat, or seaweed. Experience the memory or imagined scene from without, in the role of an observer, as you do this.

Step 3. Once all the different parts are in place, enter the memory or imagined scene and experience it from within. Take in the whole sensation.

Step 4. Just as the emotion's strength is peaking, plant your anchor (make a fist and say "Never give up!" or whatever seems appropriate). Maintain the anchor for a moment as the emotion is peaking, then release it before the emotion ebbs out.

Step 5. Rest for a few seconds. Then repeat steps 2 to 4, but when you add the various sensory impressions, try to make everything a little stronger than before. Make the colors more intense, the noises louder, the heat warmer, and so on. This way, you will also strengthen the related emotion. If you feel the memory can't be made any stronger than it is, try a different memory that uses the same emotion. It won't make any difference. Amplify the senses and the emotion each time, and anchor in the same way as before.

Step 6. Perform step 5 three or four times, planting your anchor in the same place each time. If you've done it the right way, by now you should have created a very strong anchor in your own mind.

Step 7. Now it's time to try it out. First, get some rest. Go someplace else, so you're not in the same place where you did the exercise. Once you feel relaxed, trigger the anchor (by clenching your fist in the same way, for example). If the anchor was planted properly, you will be filled with the emotion immediately. On cue. You can't avoid it; you've just given yourself a physical reflex. It's an incredible sensation. If the emotion is weak or doesn't appear, you've either timed the anchor incorrectly or you didn't manage to feel the emotion properly when you made the anchor. In which case, all you need to do is try again.

Practice, Practice, Then Practice Some More

Creating anchors in other people is a skill that takes practice to become effective. It's mostly a question of getting into the habit of it, and getting the timing right, so that you establish the anchors at the moment when the feelings are at their strongest. But it's easy to practice, just like with rapport. It's just a matter of doing it whenever you can. The idea is for this to become an automatic action in you, just like establishing rapport is. And, actually, it really is an automatic action. The only thing you're adding is the ability to choose to establish positive anchors and not negative ones, and also to be able to control what the actual anchor is to be.

Planting anchors should be fun and simple. There's no reason to use lots of different anchors for different people. Use standard anchors, and always use the same one for joy, or determination, for example. This way you won't have to remember any more than necessary. You should make a habit of using your joy anchor (a certain touch, combined with a certain word, spoken a certain way) the moment somebody is very happy, no matter who it is. You will soon have put the same joy anchor in most of the people around you, and since you've been using the same one, you'll always know how to trigger it. You won't need to think about what you did for a particular person. And besides, if you always use the same anchor for the same emotion, no matter who the person is, and you've planted it in lots of people, what do you think might happen if you trigger the anchor in a room that has several of these people present? That's right: you've just triggered multiple emotions. How's that for a nice surprise!

Perhaps you still find all this anchor stuff a bit odd or mystical. If that's the case, I suspect you may have skipped the last exercise. Because it's actually very simple: you create a reflexive association in yourself or in somebody else, an association that links a behavior (the anchor) to a previous emotion. That's it. Words really can't do it much better justice. To understand how well it works, you have to go out and try it yourself.

Remember, just like when you practiced rapport, you can't really ever have a "negative" result. The worst that can happen is that you don't manage to establish the anchor very well and that nothing happens when you try to trigger it. You simply have to keep at it until you get the knack. When you succeed you will be making yourself and others feel happy, filled with creativity, and all the other positive emotions that you've anchored, like a good little cunning, thought-manipulating mastermind.

Your basic mind-reading training is almost over. Because of your knowledge of rapport, dominant senses, and subtle emotional expressions, you are now aware of what people are actually saying to you, what they're thinking, and what they're really feeling. You can tell when somebody tries to hide that they're feeling pressured or being untruthful. You can easily interpret and respond to unconscious signs of acknowledgment and interest that you see in others. You've also mastered techniques for implanting ideas, opinions, values, and thoughts into the minds of others, and for the same reason, you are more alert to people who do these things to you. You know how to use anchors to get yourself into the exact emotional state you want to be in, and you can do the same to the people around you.

But there's something missing.

You can't call yourself a mind reader unless you can prove to people that you can read their minds. To finish, I will therefore teach you some neat mind-reading demonstrations that you can use to impress people. So get your mesmeric stare ready, cue the dramatic music, and light the red lights. The stage is yours.

11

Show Off

IMPRESSIVE DEMONSTRATIONS
AND PARTY TRICKS

*In which you learn some delightful mind-reading
tricks that you can use to impress your friends and
cause fear and panic wherever you go.*

Thought reading as a form of entertainment is a little different from the everyday variety, of course. But for once, there won't be lots of new techniques to learn, because these demonstrations are all based on the methods (or variations of them) that you've learned in this book. The only difference is that we present them differently than before, and to far more spectacular results. Just as with everything else, these tricks will take practice to give good results. Don't expect to manage all the demonstrations perfectly the first time you try them. There's no such thing as a free lunch. But with some patience, you won't have any trouble mastering them. In fact, without being aware of it, you've already started practicing some of them.

Just remember that these demonstrations can have a very strong impact on the people who experience them. You know what you can and can't do, but your participants won't know the true limit of your "powers." Feel free to explain that you can't see straight into their minds or manipulate them at will—not quite. These party tricks can make you either a very popular person or extremely lonely, depending on how you handle the reactions of your friends and family.

Visible Thoughts

You know the thought somebody has in her mind.

This demonstration is basically about getting someone to think of an image, a sound, or a feeling. By secretly observing her eye movements, you can see which of the options she is thinking of. As you've probably realized, this involves using the EAC model from pages 63–64, to determine which thought she has in her mind. We needn't concern ourselves with whether the model is scientifically valid or not. For this trick to work, it is enough that you know what to look for. It's a really simple trick, but it can have quite a shocking impact on the person you perform it for.

The following example is not intended to be repeated word for word. I've written it to allow me to explain the different stages of the demonstration in a clear way. When you've understood the principle, it's up to you to pick suitable "themes" or thoughts to use. But for the time being, let's imagine that you're in some social situation where there are several other people around. Just one would be enough, of course, but there's no harm in having an audience. Let's imagine that someone has volunteered to take part in an interesting experiment in mind reading. You start out like this:

We're going to conduct an experiment in mind reading. Thoughts are obviously very personal things, so we'll stick to thoughts that we'll create now, together. That way I'm certain not to uncover any private thoughts that you've been having. Just relax and

follow my instructions. . . . Are you ready? Then let's begin!
Here comes the first thought. I want you to visualize your liv-
ing room as clearly as you can. Do it now. Visualize the room.
Try to include as many details as you can—furniture, pictures—
build up an image of the whole room. . . .

Here, check for definite eye movements, for instance up and to
the left. Any sign will work, as long as it is clear and consistent.

Good. Now you can erase that image. Instead, I want you to
imagine the chorus of your favorite song. Take your time.
I want you to really hear the music or the tune playing in your
head.

Now check for a clear (and different) sign for sound: for instance, the eyes to one side, and perhaps even the head to one side.
If you don't get a good reading for sound, perhaps because your
participant isn't very tonal, just continue with a kinesthetic question as though nothing happened. Remember, your volunteer and
the people watching you have no idea where this is going.

Let the music fade now. The last thing I want you to think about
is how it feels to take a shower. Feel the nice warm water spraying
over your body, feel the slippery floor or the bathtub under your
feet. . . .

Now that you have noted eye signs for at least two of the three
senses, you can ask her to go through the sensory experiences once
more if you like, to make sure that her eye movements are consistent. If you don't seem to get the same readings in the control
round, tell her that it's important that she *see* the room clearly, and

feel the water against her skin (or whatever you've chosen), so that she doesn't suddenly change her sensory experience of the different impressions you have given her. But if you have picked up some good, clear eye movements, you can proceed.

> *OK, now you've got some randomly selected, but quite different thoughts in your mind. Next, I want you to think of one of these: the living room or the shower.* [Or one of the three, if you got good readings for all three.] *Don't tell me which one you've chosen; think about one of those two. If it's the room, you can see it clearly in front of you again, and if it's the shower, you can feel the warm water on your skin again. . . .*

Now, all you need to do is pay attention to which way her eyes move, since that reveals what she's thinking of. Tell her what thought she is concentrating on. Prepare for screams. Let her try a few more times, and freak her out every time by always being able to read her mind.

Remember: throughout the demonstration, what's going on will be very obvious to you, but believe me, it won't be to anyone else. No one knows where you're headed when you ask about the different sensory experiences, and any onlookers will merely be watching an interesting process. Your volunteer won't know that she is moving her eyes, just as you probably weren't before we discussed the EAC model. When we think, we are focused internally, and have no idea of what our bodies are doing. We know still less of what we're doing with our faces, which, of course, we can't even see.

The previous example involving rooms and showers would probably be a little strange if you tried to replicate it word for word. I just used it to demonstrate the principle. Because your choice is entirely free, as far as the different impressions are concerned, you can make the mind reading as personal and intimate as you like. The trick is just to divide the impressions into visual, sound, and sensual/physical sensations. One example for very good friends might be (in somewhat truncated form):

> *I want you to see your current boyfriend clearly in front of you. . . . Now I want you to hear the voice of your last boy-friend as he speaks to you. . . . And now I want you to remember what it was like when you hugged your very first boyfriend. . . . Now I want you to think of the one of these three men that you love the most, just as you did a moment ago, but don't say anything. . . .*

The possibilities are endless. The important thing here is for you to understand the principle. After that, you're only limited by your imagination as to the sorts of thoughts you choose to use. In many situations it's probably best to use impersonal thoughts, of objects or music. But if you think the situation and the company are right for it, you can use something like the last example to make the whole experience a lot more entertaining; let your volunteer choose the thought she has the most emotional involvement in. The thought that means the most to her, what she most wants to do, what she's the most afraid of, and so on.

The good thing here is that you don't actually need to know the contents of the thoughts. You don't need to know what her favorite song is or what her boyfriend looks like in order for this to work. You just need to pay attention to how the eyes are moving. What makes this demonstration so effective is that your volunteer can think about things that are never revealed to you—yet you can still tell her what she's thinking about.

A Bird in Hand

You know which hand an object has been concealed in.

This demonstration involves you repeatedly guessing which hand somebody has hidden a small object in. I will give you three different ways of doing this. I suggest you do this in sequence, and use a new method each time you repeat the demonstration. The more times you can repeat this, the more impressive it gets, since you do have a 50 percent chance of getting the first attempt right after all.

If you do it three times, one incorrect guess won't hurt you too much, either. After all, this mind-reading stuff is difficult. Apart from demonstrating mind reading, you will give a demonstration of influence and control. Your participant will, to everyone else's delight, and his own mild frustration, be completely defenseless in your hands.

The basic setup is to ask somebody to conceal a small object in one of his hands. Something you can hold inside your hand, like a ring, coin, rock, or a piece from a game. Then, you ask him to put both hands behind his back. Explain to him that he is free to switch hands as he likes, then he should choose which hand he will finally conceal the object in. When he has decided on a hand, ask him to close both hands into fists, behind his back, and then bring them out, in front of his body. Let the games begin!

The First Test

This method is a good one to begin with, as it is almost embarrassingly simple. All you need to do is use your ability to observe subtle physical changes in your volunteer. When he is holding his hands behind his back, switching the object back and forth between his hands a couple of times, you stand with your back to him. Ask him to hold his empty hand straight out, and raise the hand with the object to his temple.

This might sound strange, but I want you to fill your thoughts with feelings, the sensation of this hand. Take a couple of seconds to create a mental image of it, and then imagine it filling up your entire brain.

What you're really after is to get him to hold his hand to his temple for five to seven seconds. The things you're saying are just there to mask this fact.

Ready? Then you can take your hand down again, and put it next to the other one. . . . Do it NOW.

Right after you say "now," you turn around and take a quick look at her hands. Don't turn around too soon. You don't want your audience to believe you snuck a peek while he lowered his arm. Give his hands a quick glance; that's all you'll need. One of the hands will be much paler than the other one. It hasn't had the same blood flow, because it was held up to the temple, so you know that the pale hand is the one with the object in it. But don't give this away at once.

To deepen the mystery, you should wait until the hands are both the same color again. After having quickly checked to see which hand it is, you look your volunteer in the eyes and are silent for a few moments, before dramatically revealing which hand holds the object.

I can see it clearly; there is a crystal clear image in there . . . an image of your . . . right hand! Open your right hand, please.

The Second Test

This time, your volunteer will be perfectly still, which will make the trick all the more astounding. This method demands more of your observational skills, however. Ask her to hold her arms extended in front of her and to look straight ahead. Make sure her arms are high enough and close enough together so that both of her arms are within her immediate field of vision. Now ask her to concentrate hard on the hand holding the coin or other object, without giving anything away, then wait for a few seconds.

If you're lucky, you may already have seen a slight twist of the head, or even a quick glance, at the hand holding the object. These movements can be very small, however.

Here's a tip: look to see if the tip of her nose starts pointing in either direction. If you observe any such movement, you can end it here and reveal which hand has the object. If not, you can proceed by asking her to create an image of the hand in her mind and to visualize it clearly in front of her. She won't be able to resist taking a quick, almost undetectable look at the correct hand. It's in the periphery of her field of vision, and the temptation to just take a quick look at it will be too big to resist. This will either happen unconsciously, after which you mind-read your way to finding the object, or she will realize that you made her look, which is a good reaction, too. After all, this is mind reading and *influence* we're dealing with here.

Ask her to place her hands behind her back again, to switch the object around a few times. When she's done, just as before, you ask her to extend her arms with closed fists.

The Third Test

The last method is completely based on suggestion. If you're not sure it will work, have somebody try it on *you* first. You'll see it works really well. It's a true classic in the world of suggestion. Your participant has switched the object around for the last time and is holding her arms out again. On the first couple of attempts, the angle of the arms wasn't such a big matter, but now you ask her to hold her arms straight out, parallel to the floor. Then ask her to close her eyes. This is the first stage of the suggestion:

> *I'm going to tell you a couple of things. All you need to do is listen. Try to imagine what I am saying as well as you can, but make sure not to move your arms. Hold them absolutely still. OK? Now, relax. . . . Good. Now I'd like you to imagine the object you're holding slowly getting heavier . . . and heavier . . . and heavier. It's as though it were made of solid lead. . . . It's getting so heavy you can barely hold it anymore. . . . Feel it getting heavier. . . . It's twice as heavy as it was when we started. . . .*

You should have a result by this point: one of the participant's arms will sink toward the floor. As soon as you see a small motion in one hand, small enough that only you can see it, you can end the demonstration with mind reading if you want:

> *Why not just open your right hand and let that awful heavy object fall out?*

The spectators, who will have been a few feet away, will swear the hand never moved. But if this is your last demonstration, you might as well make it a really powerful one, and continue with the next step:

Now I'd like you to imagine that there is a string tied to your other arm. At the other end of that string, there is a helium balloon. It's a big balloon, and it's making your hand feel so light . . . so light. It doesn't weigh a thing; it wants to fly. . . . The balloon is trying to lift you toward the ceiling . . . but you're held in place by the lump of lead in your other hand, which just keeps getting heavier. . . . In fact, by now you're actually holding a whole bucket of those heavy lumps of lead. . . .

Keep making one hand heavier and the other one lighter. In the end, the participant will be standing there with her arms wide apart, one pointed down and the other one pointed up, like a big letter "K." How far apart the arms go will vary from person to person, but it is very rare for the difference to be too small to notice.

Keep your eyes closed for a while longer. Have you felt your arms move at all?

The answer will be no. If there are other people present, ask them to state out loud which hand they believe the object is hidden in. The spectators won't have any trouble knowing which hand it is, of course.

Keep your eyes closed, and stand still. [You don't want her hands to start moving too early.] *Is it true that the object is in your right hand? Since you haven't moved your arms, all our spectators must be mind readers, too. Right? Open your eyes.*

Your participant will be very surprised to see her arms point in two completely different directions, instead of straight ahead. Take a bow, and don't forget to tell the audience to give your participant a hand, too!

Back and Forth

A Classic of the Supernatural
with a Natural Explanation

I had to think long and hard before deciding to include this section here. I was afraid it would be dismissed as nonsense, destroy the book's credibility, and make people throw it out of the nearest open window. But I figured that if you're still reading this, you have the knowledge you need to be capable of realizing that it's no stranger than anything else, and it works by the same principles as everything else in this book. I'm talking about . . . pendulums.

Yep, pendulums.

Those patchouli-scented hippie crystals on a string that people with henna-dyed hair claim can reveal your future fortunes. Pendulums. But, actually, pendulums work according to the psychophysiological principle that says that all of our thoughts have some effect on our bodies. Before you dismiss this as utter nonsense, I'd like you to please at least try this out, empirically, and get an understanding for what it is you're dismissing. If you don't, you're just being superstitious. I understand if you're experiencing doubts and feeling very skeptical right now. But please trust me.

Convince Yourself

Get a piece of string, about eight inches long, and tie a ring or something similar to one end of the string. It should be an object of some weight, at least. If the object is too light, the pendulum won't work as well. Then draw a circle, about six inches across, on a sheet of paper. Draw a vertical line through the middle of the circle, and write "YES" next to the line. Then draw a horizontal line through the circle, and write "NO" next to it. Or use the circle printed below.

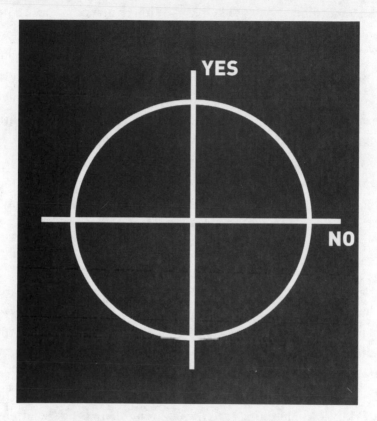

Hold the loose end of the string between your thumb and index finger. Let the pendulum rest above the intersection of the lines, at the center of the circle. This is always the starting position. Now lift the pendulum, so that it is hanging straight over the intersection of the crosshairs. Concentrate on the YES line. Think, "YESYESYESYES" to yourself, loud and clear—and notice the pendulum beginning to move back and forth over the line! Make an effort not to move your hand. You can support it with your other hand to give it more stability. As you have noticed, it doesn't make any difference. The pendulum will keep moving back and forth along that line. Now switch to the NO line, instead. Concentrate and think, "NONONONO." Without any conscious action on your part, the pendulum will suddenly change direction! Now, it will follow the NO line instead. Make sure you're still keeping your hand still. Now think "CIRCLE," and see how the pendulum starts making a circular motion over the paper instead. Alternate between YES, NO, and CIRCLE a few times, until you're convinced.

It's all because of something called *ideomotor responses*. When you think, you unconsciously cause small-scale muscle reactions that the human eye can't detect. But when amplified by the length of the string and the weight of the pendulum, they're suddenly very obvious.

The pendulum feels "magical" because we can see it move, despite the person who is holding it swearing, and us seeing, that his hand is completely still. Perhaps that makes it seem reasonable to ascribe the movements of the pendulum to some arcane cause or other. Books about pendulums never wait long to introduce colorful concepts like "Holy Guardian Angel" or "magical force of the pendulum." My ambition isn't to make the world a less-interesting place by claiming there is no such thing, but I think it's unnecessary to look any further for an explanation than to our own physiological responses. The best explanation of how the pendulum works that I've read was formulated by pendulum experts Greg Nielsen and Joseph Polansky, veterans of the business:

The human nervous system . . . is the communication system of the body. Through the nervous system the brain gets all its data

from the internal organs, and then transmits the appropriate
messages back to those organs. . . . It is not the pendulum itself,
therefore, which is giving you the answers. It is your higher in-
telligence communicating through the nervous system—which
gives you signals.

OK, I admit that it's not obvious that the unconscious mind is a higher intelligence. But, as they say, close enough. So the reason why we only see the pendulum move and not the hand, is that the pendulum amplifies the small, undetectable motions of the hand, muscle reactions that are too small for us to even notice and that are beyond our conscious control. The idea of ideomotoric responses is not news; it was first expressed in 1852 by psychologist William B. Carpenter, who also invented the actual term "ideomotor action." The idea was clarified by the famous philosopher and psychologist William James, who I mentioned previously, in 1890:

Whenever movement follows unhesitatingly and immediately
the notion of it in the mind, we have ideo-motor action. . . . [I]t
is no curiosity, but simply the normal process. . . .

Apparently, nobody was listening. The seemingly mystical powers of the pendulum, and people's ignorance of how and why it works, have caused some incorrect ideas about what it can meaningfully be used for. It's a popular alternative to dowsing rods, for finding lost objects. This could work, but only if you unconsciously know where the object is, even though you've forgotten it for the moment. Like where you put your car keys. But holding one over a map to try to find missing people—which has both been suggested and done—just doesn't make sense. If it should actually work, that would only indicate that the person holding the pendulum actually did have information about the missing person's whereabouts. And if that's the case, you're probably in bad company.

And now that you know the pendulum doesn't need to interact with the spirit world, or with ley lines, to work, and that it's really no more mysterious than any other bodily reaction you have when you think of something, you can go pick this book up from the lawn outside of your window. Now the time has come for you to mystify people with your discoveries about the pendulum.*

The First Test

Instruct your participant how to hold the pendulum, and explain about the starting position at the crosshairs inside the circle. If she wants to stop the pendulum, she can lower it to the crosshairs again, but she should never stop the pendulum with her other hand. Use the same circle with the YES and NO lines as before.

When you're experimenting with pendulums, a circular motion means "doubt" or that there will be no answer given. Begin by having your participant think "YES," "NO," and "CIRCLE," just like you did before, to show her how it works. This will also give you an opportunity to determine how large this person's reactions are, and how long it takes for the pendulum to change direction. Be careful to explain to the participant that she shouldn't move her hand at all.

In the first test, you choose a question that is answered with a

---

* My editor would like to point out that if you actually did throw the book out of the window, you wouldn't be able to read my suggestion that you go out to get it back. He's right of course. You should never throw this book anywhere, no matter what I say.

number, that your participant knows the answer to, but not you. For example:

How many cups of coffee did you drink today?
How many guys did you chat up last night at the bar?

Ask her to lift the pendulum from the circle, hold it still, and say: "Ten." (You should begin with a guaranteed NO. Depending on the question you choose, you may need to use a higher number; look at the examples just given.) Wait until the pendulum responds along the NO line.

How soon the pendulum will respond depends on the person; it could be immediate and very clear, or just a cautious little bit of motion. Once you have the first NO, continue to count down, while keeping your eyes on the pendulum. Pause at each number, to give the pendulum a chance to change directions: *Nine. Eight. Seven. Six. Five. Four. Three. Two. One. Zero.*

At one of the numbers, the pendulum will suddenly change directions and begin to move along the YES line. The number where the pendulum changes directions is the correct answer to your question. Ask your participant if she moved her hand at all. She'll say no. Ask her if the number was the right one. She'll say yes.

Interlude

Feel free to explain how the pendulum works after you've performed the first test. Explain that it is controlled by tiny muscular activities we are unaware of, that our nervous system controls them, and that the pendulum amplifies them. The other experiment will only be all the more interesting, especially for your test subject, if everybody understands the mechanisms involved.

The Pendulum as a Lie Detector

Use the pendulum as a lie detector. This is simply a visual example of unconscious contradictory signs, like you read about in chapter 7 on lying. Your participant will try to say one thing with his words, but his body will signal something else, and the pendulum will amplify it.

Let's say you're in a room with five people besides you and your participant. Ask him to rest the pendulum on the crosshairs, and silently pick one of the people in the room. He's going to think of this person during the experiment. Explain that you're going to speak the names of everybody who is present, one after the other. For each person, you will ask if this is the person your participant is thinking of. He is to answer no every time, even when it's the right person. When you're sure he's chosen somebody, and that he's understood the instructions, you ask him to pick the pendulum up. Just as in the previous experiment, you will begin with a certain outcome, to make sure he's "playing along."

Mention somebody who isn't present, and ask if that is the person he picked. Wait for the NO from the pendulum. If you're working with somebody who only gives small responses, you can, if you need to, ask about another person who isn't present. Once you have a good, clear response, you continue with the five people in the room: *Is it Harry? Is it Ron?* And so on. Your test subject is supposed to answer "NO" to each question, but one of the questions—*Is it Hermione?*—will make the pendulum swing over to YES, irrespective of what the test person herself is claiming. The pendulum will reveal his lie without fail. (For this reason, you should make sure the lie concerns a trivial matter, so there aren't any bad feelings afterward, when everybody has left the party because of the two people arguing in the kitchen, and you end up renting a bad movie with Ben Stiller in it and consuming an entire bag of potato chips and a huge bottle of Coke.)

I hope you will be brave enough to try out these demonstrations or experiments. Most of them are easier to perform than you think. All they require is that you use the skills you've already been practicing, for you to have faith in yourself, and, perhaps at first, no matter whether you're a woman or a man, you will need some massive *co jones.*

12

Mind Reading!!

SOME FINAL THOUGHTS ABOUT WHAT YOU'VE LEARNED

In which you find you're a qualified mind reader,
the author tells you of his disappointments concerning the
future, and our journey comes to an end.

We've finally reached the end. If you've actually done all the exercises and mastered each section of the book before moving on, it has most likely taken you several months to get here. If, instead, you've done what I tend to do and just read the book from beginning to end without stopping for the exercises, that's OK, too. One of the great things about books is you can skip from page to page as it suits you. The exercises and methods aren't going anywhere. It doesn't matter if you've already begun training your mind-reading abilities or are about to begin doing so. In either case, I hope I have convinced you of one thing: THIS *IS* MIND READING. MIND READING IS NO MYTH. It just happens to be a little different than what most people imagine. *Reading* is, per definition, something we do with our eyes (even though some can read with their fingertips). Then we have to be able to *see* the thing we're reading. And what we can see is the ways our thought processes affect our bodies and our behavior. Since Descartes was wrong, what we see is actually also an integrated part of the thought process in question, which also allows us to deduce the rest with relative ease.

I am sometimes asked what will happen when everybody knows how to do this. Of course, it would be weird if everybody went around consciously analyzing each other all the time. "Hey there, nice to meet you. Do you want to follow my body language first, or shall I start?" But as I've told you over and over, your learning is not complete until you're doing all these things unconsciously again.

And once we've all learned these techniques, what then? Well, I guess we'll be better people for the simple reason that we are paying attention to each other instead of to ourselves. We'll move through our lives with fewer frictions and have more fun. There will still be differences of opinion, but actual conflicts will often be solved in their early stages, in pleasant and respectful meetings. We will probably prevent a war or two from ever being started. (On the other hand, I think that in the future we will all wear silver leotards and live in colonies on Mars. I have recently begun to wonder if perhaps those magazines I read when I was young were full of lies. . . .) I guess the problem is that this will never happen, though. There will always be people who don't want to be in rapport with others, and who are fully content to struggle through life using concealed suppression techniques. Fortunately, we can resist them and manage without them, once we understand what we're really thinking of and expressing when we communicate with each other.

With the toolbox you have been given, you can know a whole lot about somebody you've never met before within a few seconds. You will know which sensory impressions she uses to understand the world. That means you will know which kinds of experiences are significant to her.

You will be able to draw conclusions about her probable interests or occupation. When you notice the things that happen in her face, you'll see what her emotions are or how her emotional state is changing. When her thinking changes, you will notice it immediately, through changes you observe in her body language and facial expressions. If there is a negative change in her emotional state, you can deflect it with no more than a word, probably before she's even aware of what is about to happen. You can immediately detect any dishonesty or lies. You smile to yourself about how her colleague is attracted to her, but neither one of them seems to notice it.

Within a few seconds, you know more about how she functions and how she thinks than many of her friends do. If that's not mind reading, I'm not sure what is. Since you're paying attention to how she uses her body language and her voice when she's communicating, you're one of the few people who actually understand exactly what she's trying to say. You make sure to also use the same body language and voice and all of the information you already have about her to make your relationship one of crystal-clear communication. You are ready to create an exciting, creative atmosphere in which to talk about your ideas, and you like each other's company. Voilà.

I told you this would come in handy.

—*Henrik Fexeus*

Such too are the layers of the phrase "once upon a time," with which I deliberately started the narrative . . . it implies that any story that follows it is both true and not true. As Bettelheim observes of fairy stories: "Since it is a fairy-tale . . . the child . . . can swing back and forth in his own mind between 'It's true, that's how one acts and reacts' and 'It's all untrue, it's just a story'" (Bettelheim, 1978:31). This psychological fluidity is one which I believe is also important for the adult, even if the adult is rather more anxious about the need for difference between reality and story than the child. This fluidity of thinking is necessary to follow the types of illusion that I describe.

—from Michael Jacobs, Illusion: A Psychodynamic
Interpretation of Thinking and Belief

References

*These are the publications and websites
I have borrowed all this stuff from.*

Bandler, Richard, and John Grinder. *Frogs into Princes.* Boulder, CO: Real People Press, 1979.

———. *Patterns of the Hypnotic Techniques of Milton H. Erickson, M.D.* Santa Cruz, CA: Meta Publications, 1975.

Barret, Lisa F., 2018, *How Emotions Are Made: The Secret Life of the Brain*, Mariner Books, New York, New York.

Borgs, Martin. *Propaganda: Så påverkas du.* Stockholm: Bokförlaget Atlas, 2004.

Brockman, John, ed. "The Mathematics of Love: A Talk with John Gottman." *Edge,* 2004. www.edge.org/3rd_culture/gottman05/gottman05_index.html.

Carnegie, Dale. *How to Win Friends and Influence People.* New York: Simon & Schuster, 1981.

Center for Learning & Organizational Development. *Integrating New Employees to the Workplace.* Corvallis: Oregon State University, 2016.

Cialdini, Robert. *Influence: The Psychology of Persuasion.* New York: Quill, 1993.

Collett, Peter. *The Book of Tells.* London: Bantam Books, 2003.

Damasio, Antonio. *Descartes' Error: Emotion, Reason, and the Human Brain.* New York: G. P. Putnam's Sons, 1994.

Darwin, Charles. *The Expression of the Emotions in Man and Animals.* London: John Murray, 1872. Available online at http://darwin-online.org.uk/EditorialIntroductions/Freeman_TheExpressionoftheEmotions.html.

Ekman, Paul. *Emotions Revealed.* London: Orion Books, 2004.

————. *Telling Lies*. New York: W. W. Norton, 2001.

Ekman, Paul, and Wallace V. Friesen. *Unmasking the Face*. Malor, MA: 2003.

Ekman, Paul, and Erika Rosenberg. *What the Face Reveals*. 2nd ed. New York: Oxford University Press, 2005.

Fleming, Charles. "Insurers Employ Voice-Analysis Software to Help Detect Fraud." *Wall Street Journal*, 2004. www.wsj.com/articles/SB108474429424412744.

Gilovich, Thomas, V. H. Medvec, and Kenneth Savitsk. "The Spotlight Effect in Social Judgement: An Egocentric Bias in Estimates of the Salience of One's Own Actions and Appearance." *Journal of Personality and Social Psychology* 78, 211–222, 2000.

Goleman, Daniel. *Emotional Intelligence*. New York: Bantam Books, 1995.

Gottman, John, Robert Levenson, and Erica Woodin. "Facial Expressions During Marital Conflict." *Journal of Family Communication* 1, 35–57, 2001.

Gottman, John, and Nan Silver. *The Seven Principles for Making Marriage Work*. New York: Crown, 1999.

Guerrero, Laura K., Joseph A. DeVito, and Michael L. Hecht, eds. *The Nonverbal Communication Reader: Classic and Contemporary Readings*. Long Grove, IL: Waveland Press, 1999.

Heap, Michael, ed. *Hypnosis: Current Clinical, Experimental and Forensic Practices*. London: Croom Helm, 1988.

Harling, Ian, and Martin Nyrup. *Equilibrium*. Denmark: Spellbound Publishing, Unpublished.

Hess, Eckhard. "The Role of Pupil Size in Communication." *Scientific American* 233, 110–119, November 1975.

Hogan, Kevin. "NLP Eye Accessing Cues: Uncovering the Myth." *Journal of Hypnotism,* September 1999.

Jacobs, Michael. *Illusion: A Psychodynamic Interpretation of Thinking and Belief*. London: Whurr Publishers, 2000.

James, William. *The Principles of Psychology*. Vols. 1 and 2. New York: Dover Publications, 1950.

Johnson, R. Colin. "Lie-Detector Glasses Offer Peek at Future of Security." EE Times, 2004. www.eetimes.com/document.asp?doc_id=1148140.

Lewis, Byron, and Frank Pucelik. *Magic of NLP Demystified: A Pragmatic Guide to Communication & Change*. Portland, OR: Metamorphous Press, 1990.

McGill, Ormond. *The Encyclopedia of Genuine Stage Hypnotism*. Hollywood, CA: Newcastle Publishing, 1947.

Mehrabian, Albert. *Nonverbal Communication*. Piscataway, NJ: Transaction Publishers, 1972.

Morris, Desmond. "The Human Animal." Episode 2. England: BBC, 1994.

———. *Peoplewatching*. London: Vintage, 2002.

Nielsen, Greg, and Joseph Polansky. *Pendulum Power: A Mystery You Can See, a Power You Can Feel*. Rochester, NY: Destiny Books, 1977.

Oatley, Keith, and Jennifer M. Jenkins, eds. *Understanding Emotions*, Oxford, UK: Blackwell Publishers, 1996.

O'Connor, Joseph, and John Seymour. *Introducing NLP*. London: Mandala, 1990.

Packard, Vance. *The People Shapers*. New York: Bantam Books, 1977.

Proust, Marcel. Remembrance of Things Past., Vol. 1: *Swann's Way*. 1922. Available online at www.gutenberg.org/files/7178/7178-h/7178-h.htm.

Ramachandran, V. S., and Sandra Blakeslee. *Phantoms in the Brain*. New York: Quill, 1999.

Richardson, Jerry. *The Magic of Rapport*. Santa Cruz, CA: Meta Publications, 2000.

Rosen, Sidney, ed. *My Voice Will Go with You: The Teaching Tales of Milton H. Erickson*. New York: W. W. Norton, 1982.

Sargant, William. *Battle for the Mind*. New York: Doubleday, 1957.

Schnoebelen, Tyler. *The Social Meaning of Tempo*. San Francisco, Spain, self-published, 2009.

Shakespeare, William. *Julius Caesar*. Available online at http://www.gutenberg.org/cache/epub/1785/pg1785-images.html.

———. *Othello*. Available online at www.gutenberg.org/cache/epub/2267/pg2267-images.html.

Steele, R. Don. *Body Language Secrets: A Guide During Courtship and Dating*. Whittier, CA: Steel Balls Press, 1999.

Vrij, Aldert. *Detecting Lies and Deceit: Pitfalls and Opportunities*. 2nd ed. West Sussex, UK: John Wiley & Sons, 2008.

Walters, Stan. *Principles of Kinesic Interview and Interrogation*. 2nd ed. Boca Raton, FL: CRC Press, 2003.

Wezowski, Patryk, and Kasia Wezowski. *Dilated Pupils and Causes Why Pupils Dilate* (video), 2013. Available as course material at centerforbodylangauge.com.

Wilson, Timothy D. *Strangers to Ourselves: Discovering the Adaptive Unconscious*. Cambridge, MA: Harvard University Press, 2002.

Winn, Denise. *The Manipulated Mind*. London: Octagon Press, 1983.

Zimbardo, Philip, and Ebbe Ebbesen. *Influencing Attitudes and Changing Behavior*. New York: Addison-Wesley, 1970.

Zuker, Elaina. *Creating Rapport*. Boston: Course Technology, 2005.

About the Author

Daniel Stigefelt

HENRIK FEXEUS is an internationally bestselling author, lecturer, mentalist, and star of several TV shows. An expert in psychology and communications, he travels the world "reading minds" and teaching others how to understand and manipulate human behavior through body language and persuasion. Henrik has studied mental skills like NLP, hypnosis, acting, and magic. You can find him on YouTube and Facebook or visit his website at www.henrikfexeus.se